'This book depicts a glimpse of EMI practice in Mexico's higher education institutions, which can enrich the contents of EMI researches in the world's non-English-speaking countries, especially in Spanish-speaking countries in Latin America.'
— *Zhiguo Zhang, College of Foreign Languages,*
Shanghai Maritime University, China

Professional Development for EMI Faculty in Mexico

Despite Mexico's implementation of a bilingual model in its tertiary education programmes, this book is the first contribution to knowledge regarding EMI in Mexico.

The author introduces readers to the Mexican higher education context before providing detailed information regarding the technological and polytechnic subsystem, where EMI has been implemented since 2012. The volume details a pilot and case study conducted in Mexican universities as well as the research findings and conclusions. It closes with recommendations, as well as suggestions for further research. The book explores the implications for the continuous professional development and training for lecturers in the current shift to EMI in Bilingual, International, and Sustainable (BIS) universities.

This volume will be of particular interest to researchers in EMI and bilingualism.

Myrna Escalona Sibaja is a Teacher Trainer at Grupo Educare and has been an EMI coach and teacher in a variety of institutions such as Instituto Santiago and Instituto Universitario de Tecnología y Cultura (IUTC), in Mexico.

Routledge Focus on English Medium Instruction in Higher Education

Professional Development for EMI Faculty in Mexico
The Case of Bilingual, International, and Sustainable Universities
Myrna Escalona Sibaja

To access the full list of titles, please visit: https://www.routledge.com/Routledge-Focus-on-English-Medium-Instruction-in-Higher-Education/book-series/RFEHE

Professional Development for EMI Faculty in Mexico
The Case of Bilingual, International, and Sustainable Universities

Myrna Escalona Sibaja

First published 2020 by Routledge

2 Park Square, Milton Park, Abingdon, Oxon OX14 4RN
605 Third Avenue, New York, NY 10017

Routledge is an imprint of the Taylor & Francis Group, an informa business

First issued in paperback 2021

Copyright © 2020 Myrna Escalona Sibaja

The right of Myrna Escalona Sibaja to be identified as author of this work has been asserted by her in accordance with sections 77 and 78 of the Copyright, Designs and Patents Act 1988.

All rights reserved. No part of this book may be reprinted or reproduced or utilised in any form or by any electronic, mechanical, or other means, now known or hereafter invented, including photocopying and recording, or in any information storage or retrieval system, without permission in writing from the publishers.

Notice:
Product or corporate names may be trademarks or registered trademarks, and are used only for identification and explanation without intent to infringe.

Publisher's Note

The publisher has gone to great lengths to ensure the quality of this reprint but points out that some imperfections in the original copies may be apparent.

British Library Cataloguing-in-Publication Data
A catalogue record for this book is available from the British Library

Library of Congress Cataloging-in-Publication Data
Names: Sibaja, Myrna Escalona, author.
Title: Professional development for EMI faculty in Mexico: the case of bilingual, international, and sustainable universities / Myrna Escalona Sibaja.
Description: Abingdon, Oxon; New York, NY: Routledge, [2020] | Includes bibliographical references and index.
Identifiers: LCCN 2019049123 (print) | LCCN 2019049124 (ebook) | ISBN 9780367350369 (hardback) | ISBN 9780429329418 (ebook)
Subjects: LCSH: English language—Study and teaching (Higher)—Mexico—Case studies. | English language—Study and teaching (Higher)—Spanish speakers—Case studies | Education, Bilingual—Mexico—Case studies. | English teachers—Training of—Mexico—Case studies. | College teachers—Training of—Mexico—Case studies. | Technical institutes—Mexico—Case studies. | Language and education—Mexico. | Language policy—Mexico.
Classification: LCC PE1068.M6 S53 2020 (print) | LCC PE1068.M6 (ebook) | DDC 428.0071—dc23
LC record available at https://lccn.loc.gov/2019049123
LC ebook record available at https://lccn.loc.gov/2019049124

ISBN: 978-0-367-35036-9 (hbk)
ISBN: 978-1-03-217598-0 (pbk)
DOI: 10.4324/9780429329418

Typeset in Times New Roman
by codeMantra

Contents

List of illustrations x
Preface xi
Acknowledgements xiii
List of abbreviations xiv

1 **Introduction: Mexico, English language programmes, higher education, and the implementation of EMI** 1
   Background 1
   The research context 1
      English language in Mexico: A broad view on the implementation of English language programmes in basic, secondary, and tertiary education 1
   Higher education in Mexico 4
      The General Coordination of Technological and Polytechnic universities (CGUTyP): A Mexican higher education subsystem 6
      The technician professional (TSU) and engineering: Educative models implemented at technological and polytechnic universities 6
        International classification of technological and polytechnic universities 7
        The technological universities in Mexico 7
        The polytechnic universities in Mexico 8
      The first BIS universities: The technological University of el Retoño and the Polytechnic University of Santa Rosa Jauregui. An overview. 8

The Bilingual, International, and Sustainable
(BIS) modality in technological and
polytechnic universities in Mexico 10
The BIS modality: Three pillars 10
The BIS modality: The curriculum 11
Notes 13
References 14

2 A pilot study 18
A pilot study 18
The pilot methods 18
The findings 19
References 20

3 A case study 21
Introduction 21
Summary 22
Problem statement 22
The research questions 22
Participants and participants' selection 23
A sociocultural stance 25
Validity and reliability 26
Ethical considerations 26
Data collection and research methods 27
Data analysis 27
Notes 29
References 29

4 The findings 32
*Participant's personal and professional
 characteristics 32*
*Lecturer's existing thoughts, ideas, and
 beliefs about the use of EMI 34*
*Existing professional development
 opportunities for lecturers provided by the
 BIS university 35*
*The manner and extent to which lecturers
 are currently using EMI within their class 38*
*How might professional development
 opportunities for EMI lecturers be improved 40*

5 Discussion, recommendations, and further research	42
Discussion and recommendations 42	
Further research 44	
Reference 44	
Appendix A: Current BIS technological and polytechnic universities spread in Mexico	45
Appendix B: English language proficiency considered by the CEFR in its 2001 volume	47
Appendix C: Guidelines for the Implementation of the BIS Model	49
Appendix D: The sheltered instruction observation protocol (SIOP) model	52
Appendix E: Training opportunities offered by the UTR since 2013	54
Glossary	57
Index	61

Illustrations

Figures

1.1	Map of the current twenty-nine BIS universities spread in Mexico	2
1.2	Administrative units SES	5
1.3	The BIS modality's schema	11

Tables

1.1	PRONI: cycles and learning objectives	4
1.2	EFL hours and subjects taught in English by term in a BIS modality	12
3.1	Positions or categories distinguished by the Mexican Technological Subsystem	25

Preface

During my trip to Mexico at the end of 2016, I visited the technological university where I worked for fourteen years. During informal conversations with colleagues, I realized that decision-makers had a strong desire for the university to become a bilingual institution. Initially, a personal reflection on the national movement towards bilingual universities in Mexico encouraged me to conduct this research. However, further reflections provided me with strong intrinsic and extrinsic motivations to conduct this study.

My experiences as a learner in Mexico, USA, Cuba, and the UK, as an English language teacher, as a lecturer teaching human resources, and quality management systems, among other subjects, as well as my work as a professional development planner and provider in a Mexican technological university, reinforced my interest in conducting a research, and then writing a book. In addition, reflecting on my professional experiences, I remembered that I delivered workshops for English language teachers and primary schools teachers, analysed instructional materials, participated in school innovation projects, and held a position as an English coordinator (internship) in the same technological university in central Mexico. In addition, I was involved in the development of networks that also might serve the research conducted in 2017 in terms of accessing universities. Through my experience I gained an understanding of the contextual layers surrounding the issues raised in Mexico, rewarding the implementation of EMI programmes in higher education. Moreover, I was convinced that my experience and the fact that I am Mexican could be of help to position myself as an insider in the professional community examined and identify myself with my participants (lecturers and professional development providers) in many ways, not only at the individual lecturer level but also at the school executive administration level as well.

At the individual level, for instance, like many of the participants in the case study I conducted (see Chapter 3), I learned English as a foreign language. I was also immersed in English as Foreign Language (EFL) in learning and teaching settings, and I have had teaching and work experience across this educational context (The Technological and Polytechnic Subsystem). Hence, my experiences as an English language learner and teacher developed better and more effective teaching strategies in my praxis that positively impacted on my students' learning.

Finally, conducting research, and writing a book on EMI, will improve me as an agent of change because this book, directly or indirectly, contributes to the enhancement of teachers and teaching EMI. Furthermore, this book will promote the views of lectures as well as provide knowledge in an under-researched area that is growing in importance in Mexico.

Acknowledgements

I would like to thank Patricia Saracho Martínez and Gabriela Zamarrón Pérez, Dean and Academic Director, respectively, at the Technological University of El Retoño for opening the door to the research conducted in 2017, which later developed into this book. Their interest and support gave me the opportunity to immerse myself in the BIS environment, and without them, this research would not have been possible.

I also thank the administrative staff, the academic staff, and the academic coordinators who offered me their valuable time to conduct my research in the best conditions, as well as for their generous availability whenever I needed them before, during, and after the research.

Abbreviations

BIS	Bilingual, international, and sustainable
CEFR	The Common European Framework of Reference for Languages
CENNI	National English level certification
CGUT	General coordination of technological universities (Mexico)
CGUTyP	General coordination of technological and polytechnic universities (Mexico)
CPD	Continuing professional development
CUP	Coordination of polytechnic universities (Mexico)
DGESPE	The Department of Higher Education Professionals
DGESU	The Department of Higher Education
DGP	Department of Professions
EMI	English as a medium of instruction
HE	Higher education
ISCED	The International Standard Classification of Education
PFCEB	Programme for the Reinforcement of Quality in Basic Education
PNIEB	National English Programme for Basic Education
PRONI	National English Programme
RQ	Research question
RQs	Research questions
SEP	Ministry of Education (Mexico)
SES	Ministry of Higher Education (Mexico)
SNIEE	National Interactive system for Educative Statistics (Mexico)
TecNM	The Mexican Technologic
TSU	Technician professional
TU	Technological University

UADM	The Open University of Mexico
UIS UNESCO	Institute of Statistics
UNESCO	United Nations Educational, Scientific and Cultural Organization
UPN	The National Pedagogical University
UPSRJ	Polytechnic University of Santa Rosa Jauregui
UTR	Technological University of El Retoño

1 Introduction

Mexico, English language programmes, higher education, and the implementation of EMI

Background

Tertiary education in Mexico is moving towards the global phenomenon of English as a medium of instruction (EMI). It means that classes in higher education (HE) institutions, specifically in technological and polytechnic universities, are being taught in English. This movement towards EMI was instituted by the Ministry of Education (SEP), and the General Coordination of Technological and Polytechnic universities (CGUTyP) in 2012. Hence, the first bilingual, international, and sustainable (BIS) technological university was opened in August 2012. By 2013, seven technological and polytechnic universities had implemented the BIS modality, and by 2015 there were twelve. Up to date, there are nineteen technological and ten polytechnic universities working under a BIS modality. Figure 1.1 shows a map of the current twenty-nine BIS universities spread in Mexico (Appendix A displays further information on the current BIS universities). Due to the positive acceptance of the BIS universities, it was planned to implement, at least, thirty-two universities by 2018 (SEP, 2017b [Report 533]). Nevertheless, there has been a slight delay on that.

By September 2017, by the time that my research was conducted, stakeholders (decision-makers, students, and lecturers) within BIS technological and polytechnic universities have had experienced the EMI programme for five years. Thus, the implementation of EMI in BIS universities seemed to be a timely topic for investigation.

The research context

English language in Mexico: A broad view on the implementation of English language programmes in basic, secondary, and tertiary education

In Mexico, learning English as a second language in basic education was officially included in 1926. Just to be suspended in 1932. Once a

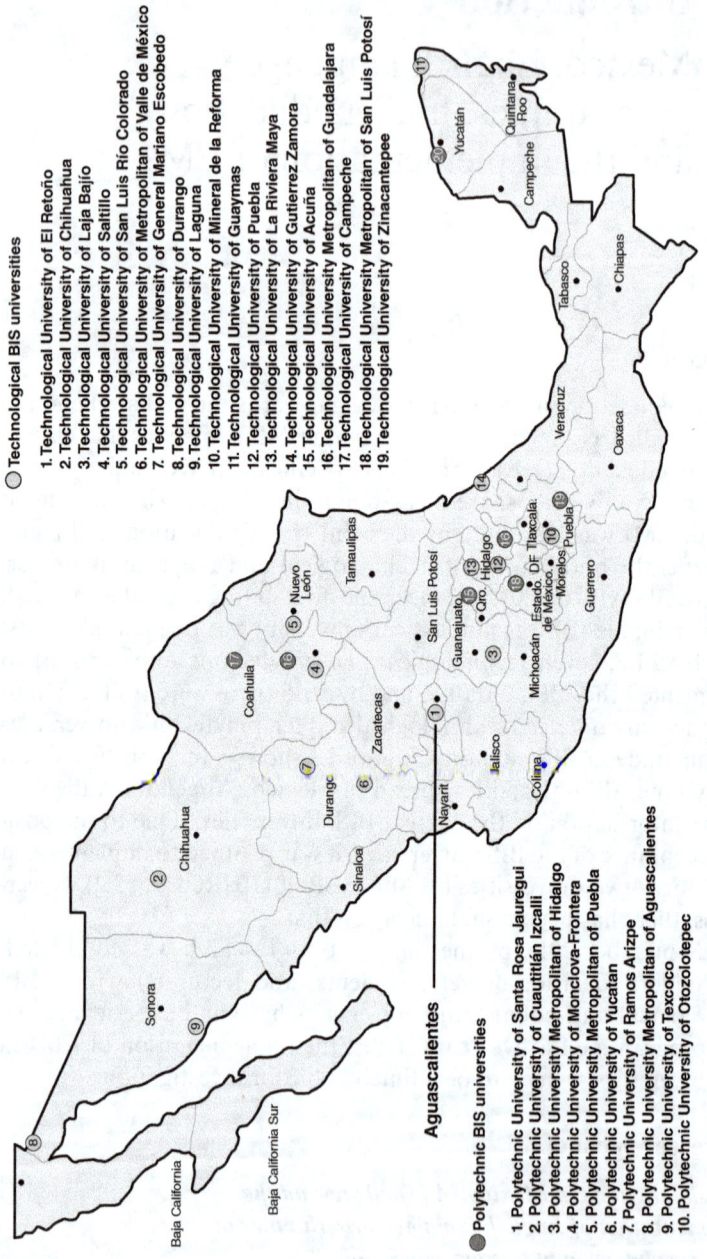

Figure 1.1 Map of the current twenty-nine BIS universities spread in Mexico.

Source: This map was developed by the author for the purpose of this book, and it is complemented with information from the BIS modality (UTR, 2017a).

new study plan was entrenched, in 1941, English was constituted in the high school curriculum[1] (Mexicanos Primero, 2015; Ramirez-Gomez et al., 2017). By 1992 local government, in a variety of states[2] such as Morelos, Nuevo Leon, Coahuila, Tamaulipas, and Sonora, made efforts towards implementing English in public preschool and primary education. These efforts concluded in 2009 when the Ministry of Education (SEP) implemented the National English Programme for Basic Education (PNIEB; Santos, 1998 as cited in Mexicanos Primero, 2015; Reyes-Cruz et al., 2011). The objective of the PNIEB was to develop a B1 English level, aligned to the Common European Framework for Languages[3] (CEFR) implemented in 2001, in learners by the time they were in secondary school (Appendix B offers further information regarding the English language proficiency considered by the CEFR in its 2001 volume). Thus, the curriculum from kindergarten to secondary school was restructured. The restructure of the curriculum involved four learning cycles. Cycle 1 focused on contact and familiarization of the English language in third (kindergarten), first, and second graders (elementary school). Cycles 2, 3, and 4 centred on developing competences to use the English language in a variety of social learning environments in third, fourth, fifth, and sixth graders in elementary school and first, second, and third graders in secondary school. The restructure of the curriculum also considered the creation of a National English Level Certification (CENNI) which aimed to provide a free-of-charge national English certification that would demonstrate that the pupils were attaining the English levels established in the curriculum, after completing the learning cycles (SEP, 2010a, 2010b, 2011a, 2011b, 2011c, 2011d).

In 2014, the PNIEB was merged with the Programme for the Reinforcement of Quality in Basic Education (PFCEB; SEP, 2017c). Unfortunately, the results of this implementation have not, officially, been provided.

By 2016, a new National English Programme (PRONI) was instigated by the SEP. Similarly to the National English Programmes implemented since 2009, the PRONI developed and implemented English language programmes for four main learning cycles (sensitize, approximate, develop, consolidate) that were aligned to the CEFR, which aimed to develop English language skills in learners at primary education (SEP, 2017c, 2018). Table 1.1 displays the four cycles and their learning objectives aligned to the CEFR.

Finally, regarding tertiary education in Mexico, the institutions have the autonomy to establish their own criteria with respect to the English language programmes, English proficiency required to potential

Table 1.1 PRONI: cycles and learning objectives

CYCLE 4 (CEFR: B1/consolidate)
Focuses on the three grades at secondary school.
Objectives of the cycle: to consolidate. The student understands and uses English language to interact in a variety of contexts.
Learning expectations: students will be able to analyse intercultural aspects, use basic and vast vocabulary in already known and current situations, interchange, and interact in social situations.

CYCLE 3 (CEFR: A2/develop)
Focuses on fifth and sixth graders at the higher elementary level.
Objectives of the cycle: to develop. The learner understands and uses English language to interact in already known contexts.
Learning expectations: students will be able to describe cultural differences amongst groups, interchange relevant and interesting information about themselves, and participate in social interchange in already known situations.

CYCLE 2 (CEFR: A1/approximate)
Focuses on third and fourth graders.
Objectives of the cycle: to approximate. The student understands and uses English language to interact in everyday situations in familiar contexts.
Learning expectations: students will be able to identify differences amongst them and other people and cultures, participate in decision-making, use information from previous experiences, and exchange personal information.

CYCLE 1 (CEFR: none/sensitize)
Focuses on kindergarten schoolers in the third grade, and the first and second graders at the lower elementary level.
Objectives of the cycle: to sensitize. The learner is sensitive to the existence of a language different from his or her mother tongue, is familiar with it, and reacts and responds to basic and personal communication needs in familiar contexts.
Learning expectations: students will be able to ask and communicate in familiar, basic contexts.

Source: The table was developed by the author based on the information obtained from the *Plan and Programmes for a Foreign Language, English, Basic Education*, published by the SEP in 2017 (SEP, 2017b, pp. 166–168).

students, as well as the English proficiency for potential graduating students. The English proficiency requirements are based on the CEFR, and they vary from A2 to C1 (Ramirez-Gomez et al., 2017).

Higher education in Mexico

The Mexican higher education (HE) system consists of three levels in four types of institutions. The first level is Higher Technical Education or Associate Professional; this educative level is better known as the

TSU level. The second level is the bachelor's degree. The third level is the master's degree and doctoral degree. The four types of HE institutions where the three levels are provided are universities (autonomous and public), technological institutes, teaching schools, and technological and polytechnic universities.

In 1976, the SEP decided to create the Ministry of Higher Education (SES). Since then, the SES has been responsible for promoting and providing quality in HE; it does it throughout its branches, officially entitled Administrative Units. These administrative units are the Department of Higher Education (DGESU), Department of Professions (DGP), General Coordination of Technological and Polytechnic universities (CGU-TyP), and Department of Higher Education Professionals (DGESPE). The SES also includes three decentralized Units, these being the National Pedagogical University (UPN), Open University of Mexico (UADM), and the Mexican Technologic (TecNM; Law for the Coordination of Higher Education, 1978; SES, 2017a, 2017b, 2017c). Figure 1.2 displays the administrative and decentralized units that belong to the SES.

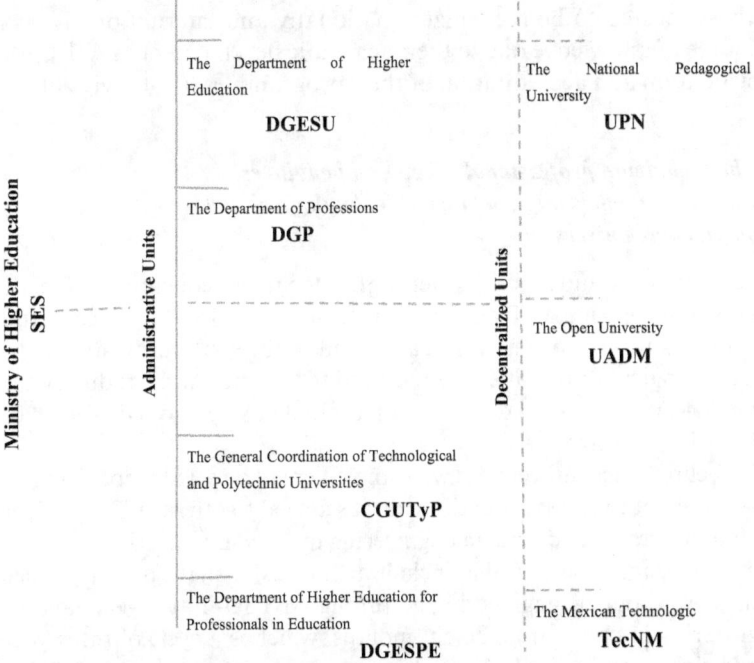

Figure 1.2 Administrative units SES.
Source: This figure was developed based on information obtained from the SES, for the purpose of this book (SES, 2017a, 2017b, 2017c).

6 *Introduction*

The General Coordination of Technological and Polytechnic universities (CGUTyP): A Mexican higher education subsystem

The General Coordination of Technological and Polytechnic Universities (CGUTyP) is one of the administrative units that belongs to the SES (see Figure 1.3). The CGUTyP aims to improve the quality of HE by developing policies, strategies, and processes that ensure the reinforcement and consolidation of the technological and polytechnic universities so that these HE institutions develop competitive human resources, as required in an economy based on knowledge (CGUT, 2010; SEP, 2014 [Report 514]).

Stakeholders at the CGUTyP foresee that the technological and polytechnic universities will be considered a HE subsystem that fulfils the expectations of both students and the society. Additionally, The CGUTyP claims that the technological and polytechnic universities will be considered competitive, with solid academic and technological basis that will let these HE institutions be linked to the industry and well integrated into the society. The technological universities are also expected to be recognized, nationally and internationally, as a source of knowledge due to their academic development as well as the evaluation and accreditation of their programmes (CGUTyP, 2017).

The technician professional (TSU) and engineering: Educative models implemented at technological and polytechnic universities

Technological universities offer higher technical education, officially known in Mexico as Technician Professional or TSU. A TSU is studied in six terms (four months each), and in the sixth-term, students at technological universities are required to practice in the industry sector. After two years, students get a diploma as TSU (CGUTyP, 2002; Ruiz-Larraguivel, 2011).

Technological universities were implemented on a TSU model and did not attempt to change it until there was a need to offer the TSU holders an undergraduate degree in engineering in 2009. Engineering is studied in 5 four-month periods that include an internship in the industry. Then, those who pursue engineering go through a TSU in two years and engineering in one year and eight months, which is a cycle of three years and eight months (De la Garza Vizcaya, 2003; Ruiz-Larraguivel, 2016).

With respect to polytechnic universities, they offer a TSU, engineering, and a technological speciality. The TSU is studied in seven terms that include two 120- and 480-hour internships in the industry, services, or educational sectors. Whereas engineering is studied in ten terms that involve two 120- and 600-hour internships. The polytechnic universities also offer a technological speciality, which is studied in one year (CUP, 2012; De la Garza Vizcaya, 2003).

Although the technological and polytechnic universities offer undergraduate technical education, there is one main difference between them; polytechnic universities offer TSU and engineering as separate studies. While in the technological universities, students should be granted with the TSU diploma if they want to be accepted for engineering.

International classification of technological and polytechnic universities

According to the International Standard Classification of Education[4] (ISCED), both TSU and engineering studies offered by the technological and polytechnic universities are "labelled as short-cycle tertiary education" and belong to a 5B and 5A levels, respectively. Levels 5B and 5A aim to provide a "high level of complexity and specialisation" (ISCED, 2011, pp. 46, 74–75, 83). Further information regarding the international classifications described by the ISCED on Technician Professional and Engineering levels can be found at UNESCO Institute of Statistics (UIS) ISCED 2011 and 2013.

The technological universities in Mexico

In 1989, the Ministry of Education (SEP) started an evaluation programme towards the improvement of HE in Mexico in both public and private universities. Additionally, the SEP investigated on the academic options being offered in HE institutions in countries such as France, Germany, England, the USA, and Japan. The SEP also conducted a research, coordinated by Dr Philip H. Coombs[5] titled "Strategy to improve the quality of higher education in Mexico" in 1991. A report on this research was developed by the International Commission for the Development of Education and submitted to the SEP (CGUT, 2010). Simultaneously, the SEP approved a project to develop a new academic option for HE that would fulfil the requirements of the industry where there was a need of workers and supervisors with more practical technical and communicative skills (CGUT, 2010; SEP, 1991).

Based on the evaluation programme, the research coordinated by Coombs, the project to develop a new academic option for tertiary education, as well as the requirements from the industry, the SEP concluded that it was timely to implement an academic option focused on the technological development linked to the needs of the industry sectors located in Mexico (SEP, 2015 [Report 233]) to both fulfil the requirement of the industry and offer jobs to undergraduates (CGUT, 2010; SEP, 1991).

The technological universities, then, emerged with three main objectives. The first, to favour marginalized communities, and decentralized HE. Second, to enlarge and diversify the academic offer to provide education linked with the socioeconomic reality as well as the dynamics of the local industry. Third, the need to link up the academy with the industrial sector in order to respond to the requirements of an emerging economy that needed well-prepared human resources (CGUT, 2010, p. 24; SEP, 1991, pp. 1, 2).

Thus, based on the main objectives discussed previously, in 1991, the first technological universities were opened in the states of Aguascalientes, Estado de México, and Hidalgo. However, due to the demand mainly from the industry sector, in 2017 there were 173 technological and polytechnic universities, 21 of them working under a BIS modality (Nuño, 2017; SEP, 2017a [Report 421]). Furthermore, these universities offered HE and degree programmes to about 163,506 students and employ almost 12,000 lecturers in one capacity or another (SNIEE, 2017).

The polytechnic universities in Mexico

The polytechnic universities were implemented as a new model in the Mexican HE subsystem in 2001. The implementation of the polytechnic model was encouraged by the SEP in the state of San Luis Potosí in 2001. The first polytechnic university is located, then, in San Luis Potosí. The next three polytechnic universities opened in 2002, the Polytechnic University of Hidalgo, and in 2003, the Polytechnic Universities of Aguascalientes and Zacatecas. These last three polytechnic universities emerged based on the Technological Academic Model implemented for technological universities in 1991 (De la Garza Vizcaya, 2003).

The first BIS universities: The technological University of el Retoño and the Polytechnic University of Santa Rosa Jauregui. An overview.

The Technological University of El Retoño (better known as the UTR) is located in El Llano in the state of Aguascalientes, north-central Mexico. It was opened in August 2012 as a branch of the Technological

University of Aguascalientes (UTA). In February 2013, it became autonomous. By 2017, there were five schools in the institution that aimed to provide qualified professionals to the local and international business community, including industry and commerce. Then, the first academic offer focused on:

- Business.
- Human resources.
- English language teaching.
- Technologies for information and communication.
- Mechatronics.

In 2017, there were 50 lecturers working for the UTR, who came from a variety of disciplines and backgrounds (UTR, 2017b) and taught to 776 students in an English language environment.

Furthermore, the UTR has implemented a Continuing Professional Development (CPD) programme that includes courses such as teaching based on competencies, micro-teaching, class planning, and English courses to improve English language skills in the lecturers and reinforce the use of EMI. Finally, since the time UTR was opened, more than 227 students have had the opportunity to study abroad, mainly in Canada and the USA in accordance with the BIS model (La Jornada Aguascalientes, 2016).

The Polytechnic University of Santa Rosa Jauregui (the UPSRJ), on the other hand, is located in Santa Rosa Jauregui, in the state of Querétaro, in central Mexico. The UPSRJ was opened in August 2011 as a traditional (monolingual) polytechnic university offering three educational options: physiotherapy, automotive systems, and software development. After conducting feasibility and needs analysis studies with the local industry, in 2013 the UPSRJ adopted the BIS modality. Then, it was positioned as the first BIS polytechnic university. By the time that the first pilot and research on EMI in BIS universities were conducted (see Chapters 2 and 3), there were five schools in this institution:

- Physiotherapy
- Automotive systems
- Software development
- Industrial metrology
- Visual effects and animation

In June 2017, there were thirty-two lecturers who were part of the teaching staff at the UPSRJ. These lecturers came from a variety of disciplines and backgrounds related to the schools to which they belonged.

Similarly to the UTR, the UPSRJ seeks to achieve quality in bilingual education, in order to provide bilingual professionals. Thus, the 1,240 students enrolled at that moment, developed knowledge in an English language environment (UPSRJ, 2017b).

The Bilingual, International, and Sustainable (BIS) modality in technological and polytechnic universities in Mexico

The TSU and engineering levels are an academic model underpinned by three main pillars that favour marginalized communities, enlarge and diversify the academic offer, and link up the academy with the industrial sector (CGUT, 2010, p. 24; SEP, 1991, pp. 1, 2).

However, due to the need of bilingual TSU and engineers in both the local and international industry/business located in Mexico, the need for a bilingual modality gained importance (Nuño, 2017). As a result, the first BIS technological university was opened in 2012 in the state of Aguascalientes, followed by the first BIS polytechnic university established in the state of Querétaro in 2013.

> The aim of the BIS universities in Mexico is to provide bilingual education to low income students who otherwise would have never had the opportunity to develop English language skills, access scholarships to study abroad, or have opportunities to position themselves in the international industry sector.
> (Saracho, 2017)

Up to date, nineteen more technological and ten polytechnic universities have opened campuses based on the BIS modality. By September 2016, twenty-one BIS universities offered bilingual education to 10,800 students in fourteen states in Mexico (UTR, 2017b). Furthermore, due to the constant demand from the industry to open BIS institutions in more technological and polytechnic universities in Mexico, the SEP planned to establish one BIS university in each state of Mexico by 2018. This means that by September 2018 there would have been thirty-two BIS universities spread all over the country (Nuño, 2017). Nevertheless, there has been a slight delay on that.

The BIS modality: Three pillars

The BIS modality focuses on three broad educative pillars:

- Bilingual
    BIS universities use EMI to offer content to students.

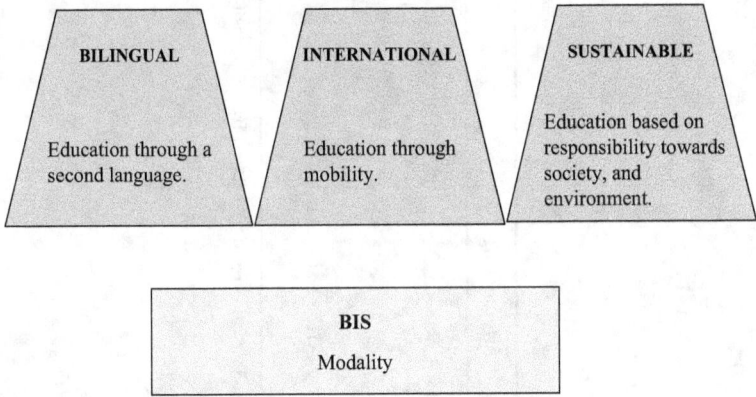

Figure 1.3 The BIS modality's schema.
Source: This figure was developed based on information obtained from the Institutional Development Plan (UPSRJ, 2017b) for the purpose of the present book.

- International
  BIS universities promote international programmes and encourage and support international mobility for the professional development and training of students and faculty members.
- Sustainable
  BIS universities offer education for sustainability. The BIS universities also promote social justice, solidarity, and responsible interaction with surrounding ecosystems (UPSRJ, 2017a, 2017b; UTR, 2017a). Figure 1.3 displays a broad schema of the BIS modality's pillars.

The BIS modality: The curriculum

The curriculum used by the BIS universities is the same curriculum developed for monolingual technological and polytechnic universities. However, the BIS modality has the following unique characteristics:

- An introductory term was implemented to immerse students into English. Students, then, attend English lessons seven hours a day; this covers 525 hours by the end of the introductory term. In addition, students are tested for their English proficiency level before and after the introductory term with the For-Real Test.[6] Students will have to prove that they hold an A2 English language level in order to start term 1. See Appendix B for further information on

Table 1.2 EFL hours and subjects taught in English by term in a BIS modality

Terms	Introductory term	TSU						Engineering				
		1	2	3	4	5	6	7	8	9	10	11
English as a foreign language (EFL) hours taught by term	525	135	135	105	75	75	Internship in the industry	75	75	75	75	Internship in the industry
Subjects taught in English	0	2	4	All	All	All		All	All	All	All	

Source: This table was developed based on the information obtained from the Educative Model (UTR, 2017b) and translated from Spanish for the purpose of the present book.

English language level(s) based on the Common European Framework of Reference for Languages (CEFR).
- In term 1, students start their formal studies. In this term, two subjects out of seven are taught in English. In term two, four subjects are taught in English. From term 3 onwards, all subjects are taught in English.
- In all terms, in addition to those subjects taught in English, students attend classes of English as a foreign language (EFL) that cover 525 hours for the TSU level and 300 hours for the engineering level (SEP, 2017b [Report 533]; SES, 2014; UTR, 2017a).

Table 1.2 shows the number of hours taught for EFL and the subjects taught using EMI by term in the BIS modality.

Then, by the end of the TSU level, students are able to study all subjects in English. This, according to the dean of the first BIS university in Mexico (Patricia Saracho), ensures that students in BIS universities attend classes where English is the medium of instruction (Arreola & Saracho, 2015).

Notes

1 Up to date, the curriculum developed for high school is not clear regarding the English proficiency level required. It broadly discusses that the students should review the most relevant learning objectives from the previous academic level (secondary) and that students are expected to have developed a more advanced English level (SEP, 2010a).
2 The state of Morelos, in central Mexico, was the first state to implement a pilot programme called English Language Teaching Programme in Primary schools in 1992. The state of Nuevo Leon started it in 1993, and the state of Coahuila in 1994. These states were followed by the states of Tamaulipas and Sonora where the programme was implemented in 2001 and 2004, respectively (Reyes-Cruz et al., 2011).
3 The Common European Framework for Languages (CEFR) was developed for three main purposes. First, to serve as a guideline to a variety of purposes such as the development of syllabuses, curriculum, examinations, and textbooks internationally. Second, to provide a clear description of what a user of the language must "learn to do… and what knowledge and skills he/she has to develop…" (CEFR, 2001, p. 1). Finally, to delineate language proficiency levels.
4 The International Standard Classification of Education (ISCED) is an international framework that assembles, compiles, and analyses statistics on education. In addition, the ISCED is the groundwork for classifying and "organizing education programmes and related qualifications by levels and fields of education" (ISCED, 2013, p. 4).
5 Dr Philip H. Coombs was the first director and founder of the International Institute for Educational Planning (IIEP) at UNESCO, and President of

the International Committee for the Development of Education (CGUT, 2010; UNESCO, 2003).
6 The For-Real Test is a downloadable placement. This test has been adopted and adapted by BIS universities for academic purposes. The For-Real Test can be retrieved from http://www.helblinglanguages.com/index.php?option=com_content&task=view&id=648&Itemid=401.

References

Arreola, H., & Saracho, P. (2015). *Noticias México al Día 16/07/15*. Retrieved 2 May 2017, from https://www.youtube.com/watch?v=lJuFP5Rl8Io.
CEF. (2001). Retrieved 29 February 2017, from https://rm.coe.int/CoERMPublicCommonSearchServices/DisplayDCTMContent?documentId=0900001680459f97.
CGUT. (2010). XV años de las universidades tecnológicas. Retrieved 15 September 2016, from http://cgutyp.sep.gob.mx/publicaciones/LibroXVUUTT/CAPITULOI/CAPITULOI.pdf.
CGUTyP. (2002). Políticas para la operación, desarrollo y consolidación del subsistema. Retrieved 17 May 2017, from http://cgutyp.sep.gob.mx/Areas/CoordAcademica/_PoliticasOperacionUT.pdf.
CGUTyP. (2017). Nosotros. (n.d.). Retrieved 20 September 2017, from http://cgut.sep.gob.mx/quienessomos.php.
CUP. (2012). Estrategias de Gestión para la Operación del MOdelo de Educación basada en Competencias. Subsistema de Universidades Politécnicas. Retrieved 1 July 2019, from http://cgutyp.sep.gob.mx/Areas/CoordAcademica/_EstrategiasGestionUP.pdf.
De la Garza Vizcaya, E. (2003). Las Universidades Tecnológicas: Un nuevo modelo en el sistema de educación superior en México *Revista de Educación Superior, 32*(126). Retrieved 2 May 2017, from http://publicaciones.anuies.mx/revista/126/2/5/es/las-universidades-politecnicas-un-nuevo-modelo-en-el-sistema-de.
ISCED. (2011). The International Standard Classification of Education. Published in 2012 by UNESCO Institute for Statistics. Retrieved 18 September 2016, from http://www.uis.unesco.org/Education/Documents/isced-2011-en.pdf.
ISCED. (2013). International Standard Classification of Education Fields of education and training 2013 (ISCED-F 2013) – Detailed field descriptions. Published in 2015 by UNESCO Institute for Statistics. Retrieved 1 September 2019, from http://uis.unesco.org/sites/default/files/documents/international-standard-classification-of-education-fields-of-education-and-training-2013-detailed-field-descriptions-2015-en.pdf.
La Jornada Aguascalientes. (2016). Se gradúan de la Universidad Tecnológica El Retoño 89 profesionales bilingües. *Redacción*, April 9. Retrieved 6 April 2017, from http://www.lja.mx/2016/04/se-graduan-de-la-universidad-tecnologica-el-retono-89-profesionales-bilingues/.

Law for the Coordination of Higher Education. (1978). Retrieved 20 February 2017, from http://www.diputados.gob.mx/LeyesBiblio/pdf/182.pdf.

Mexicanos Primero. (2015). *Sorry. Learning English in Mexico* (1st edition). Retrieved 1 June 2018, from http://www.mexicanosprimero.org/index.php/educacion-en-mexico/como-esta-la-educacion/estado-de-la-educacion-en-mexico/sorry-2015.

Nuño, A. (2017). Palabras de Aurelio Nuño – Inauguración de la Universidad Tecnológica BIS del estado de Puebla. Retrieved 17 January 2017, from https://www.youtube.com/watch?v=EJFb2otLqYg.

Ramirez-Gomez, L. A., Perez-Maya, C. J., & Lara-Villanueva, R. S. (2017). Panorama del Sistema Educativo Mexicano en la Enseñanza del Idioma Inglés como Segunda Lengua. *Revista de Cooperacion*. ISSN 2308-1953, Issue 12, June 2017. Retrieved 6 August 2019, from http://revistadecooperacion.com/numero12/012-02.pdf.

Reyes-Cruz, M., Murrieta-Loyo, G., & Hernández-Méndez, E. (2011). Políticas Lingüísticas Nacionales e Internacionales sobre la Enseñanza del Inglés en Escuelas Primarias. *Revista Pueblos y fronteras digital, 6*(2), 167–197, December 2011–May 2012. Mexico: UNAM. Retrieved 8 August 2019, from https://www.redalyc.org/pdf/906/90621701007.pdf.

Ruiz-Larraguivel, E. (2011). La educación superior tecnológica en México. Historia, situación actual y perspectivas. *Revista Iberoamericana de Educación Superior, II*(3). Retrieved 20 August 2019 from http://www.redalyc.org/pdf/2991/299124244002.pdf.

Ruiz-Larraguivel, E. (2016). De Tecnico Superior a Ingeniero. Aumentando la condición de sobreeducacion en el trabajo. Retrieved 20 August 2019, from https://www3.azc.uam.mx/sieee/cuartoseminario/ponencias/ponencia15.pdf.

Santos, A. (1998). Historia de la Educación Secundaria en México. Ynclan, Gabriela (compiler), Everything to do. Some problems with Lower Secondary School. Anthology, Mexico, SNTE Board for Mexican Teacher Culture, A.C.

Saracho P. (2017). Interview-meeting: Introduction to the BIS modality and the administrative staff at the UTR. Interview conducted by Myrna Escalona Sibaja. [Formal meeting with The Dean of the first BIS University] Technological University El Retoño, Aguascalientes. 31 July 2017 at 11:00 am. Meeting room Sala de Juntas de Rectoría.

SEP. (1991). Universidad Tecnológica. Una nueva opción para la formación profesional a nivel superior. Libro azul. Retrieved 15 September 2016, from http://transparencia2.zacatecas.gob.mx/files/LIBRO%20AZUL2010.pdf.

SEP. (2010a). Orientaciones para la Enseñanza del Inglés en el Bachillerato General. Retrieved 8 August 2019, https://www.dgb.sep.gob.mx/informacion-academica/otros/orientaciones-enzenanza-ingles.pdf.

SEP. (2010b). Programa Nacional de Inglés en Educación Básica. Second Language: English. Syllabus. Cycle 1: 3rd. Preschool, 1st. And 2nd Elementary school. Retrieved 1 June 2019, https://www.gob.mx/cms/uploads/attachment/file/92637/PNIEB-Cycle-1.pdf.

SEP. (2011a). Programa Nacional de Inglés en Educación Básica. Second Language: English. Cycle 4: 1st, 2nd, and 3rd. Secondary School. In-class testing stage. Retrieved 4 June 2019, from https://www.gob.mx/cms/uploads/attachment/file/92640/PNIEB-Cycle-4.pdf.

SEP. (2011b). Programa Nacional de Inglés en Educación Básica. Second Language: English. Curricular foundations. Preschool, Elementary school, and Secondary School. Phase of expansion. Retrieved 5 June 2019, from https://www.gob.mx/cms/uploads/attachment/file/92641/FUNDAMENTOS-PNIEB.pdf.

SEP. (2011c). Programa Nacional de Inglés en Educación Básica. Second Language: English. Guia de nivelación. Cycle 3: Fortalecimiento Académico para profesores de inglés. Phase of expansion. Retrieved 8 June 2019, from https://www.gob.mx/cms/uploads/attachment/file/16086/Guias_de_Nivelacion.pdf.

SEP. (2011d). Programa Nacional de Inglés en Educación Básica. Second Language: English. Guia de nivelación. Cycle 2: Fortalecimiento Académico para profesores de inglés. Phase of expansion. Retrieved 8 June 2019, from https://www.gob.mx/cms/uploads/attachment/file/16073/Guias_de_Nivelacion_2.pdf.

SEP. (2014). Report 514. Manual de Organización de la Coordinación General de Universidades Tecnológicas y Politécnicas. Retrieved 10 September 2017, from http://cgut.sep.gob.mx/2014/Transparencia/manuales/MO/514_MO.pdf.

SEP. (2015). Report 233. Universidades Tecnológicas y Politécnicas. Retrieved 20 December 2016, from http://www.gob.mx/sep/prensa/comunicado-233-mas-de-113-mil-visitas-registra-el-portal-unlugarparati-mx?state=published.

SEP. (2017a). Report 421. Se está en el proceso para el diálogo con la Coordinadora en sus estados: Nuño Mayer. Retrieved 26 April 2017, from http://www.gob.mx/sep/prensa/comunicado-421-se-esta-en-el-proceso-para-el-dialogo-con-la-coordinadora-en-sus-estados-nuno-mayer.

SEP. (2017b). Report 533. Universidades Tecnológicas y Politécnicas con Modelo BIS responden a demanda global de profesionistas de calidad. Retrieved 16 January 2017, from https://www.gob.mx/sep/prensa/comunicado-533-universidades-tecnologicas-y-politecnicas-con-modelo-bis-responden-a-demanda-global-de-profesionistas-de-calidad.

SEP. (2017c). Plan y programas de estudio, orientaciones didácticas y sugerencias de evaluación. Aprendizajes clave para la educación integral. Lengua extranjera. Inglés. Educación básica. Plan y programas de estudio, orientaciones didácticas y sugerencias de evaluación. Primera edición. Retrieved 13 March 2019 from https://www.planyprogramasdestudio.sep.gob.mx/descargables/biblioteca/basica-ingles/1LpM-Ingles_Digital.pdf.

SEP. (2018). Informe: Evaluación de consistencia y resultados 2017–2018. Programa Nacional de Inglés. Instancia evaluadora: El Colegio de México. Retrieved 30 January 2018 from https://www.gob.mx/cms/uploads/attachment/file/388690/Informe_Final_-_S270_Programa_Nacional_de_Ingle_s.pdf.

SES. (2014). Lineamientos para la implementación del modelo BIS en las universidades tecnológicas y politécnicas. Retrieved 10 May 2017, from https://www.gob.mx/busqueda.

SES. (2017a). Higher Education System. Retrieved 16 February 2017, from http://www.ses.sep.gob.mx/educacionsinfronteras/.
SES. (2017b). Antecedentes. Retrieved 27 February 2017, from http://www.ses.sep.gob.mx/hacemos.html.
SES. (2017c). Unidades administrativas. Retrieved 27 March 2017, from http://www.ses.sep.gob.mx/u_administrativas.html.
SNIEE. (2017). Dirección General de Planeación y Estadística Educativa. Sistema Nacional de Information Estadística Educativa. Retrieved 1 July 2017, from http://www.planeacion.sep.gob.mx/principalescifras/.
UNESCO. (2003). 40th anniversary. Retrieved 20 September 2017 from http://www.iiep.unesco.org/sites/default/files/40th_anniversary.pdf.
UPSRJ. (2017a). BIS model. Retrieved 14 September 2017, from http://upsrj.edu.mx/modelo-bis/.
UPSRJ. (2017b). Plan institutional de desarrollo. BIS modality. Retrieved 14 February 2017, from https://drive.google.com/drive/folders/0B8Vse9TAFsCYUmo3NFdyenVvVjA.
UTR. (2017a). BIS modality. Retrieved 9 February 2017, from https://www.utr.edu.mx/index.php/es/about-us/modelo-educativo.
UTR. (2017b). Tema 6. Modalidad Bilingüe, Internacional y Sustentable (BIS). Documento de trabajo para integrarse en el Libro azul de la CGUTyP. Unpublished document developed by the Academic Director at the UTR. Document to be submitted to CGUTyP.

2 A pilot study

A pilot study

At the end of 2016, I identified the need to conduct a research on English as a Medium of Instruction (EMI) at BIS universities. A natural step towards that research was to conduct a pilot study that would help to define the data collection with respect to both the content and the procedures to be followed and to develop "relevant lines of informed questioning and preparation of appropriate questions regarding the research methods" (Yin, 2009).

The pilot study was carried out in the Technological University of El Retoño (UTR) and the Polytechnic University of Santa Rosa Jauregui (UPSRJ) during May-June 2017. These BIS universities were chosen because they are the first BIS technological and polytechnic universities established in Mexico, and the author had already accessed both institutions through the Academic Directors, who had consented to be part of the pilot and research. Thus, it was both "convenient and appropriate" (Yin, 2014).

The participants in the pilot study consisted of six lecturers and six students who came from a variety of disciplines, including business, English language teaching, technologies for information and communication, and software development.

The pilot methods

Four instruments were designed: two questionnaires and two protocols for semi-structured interviews. The questionnaires were developed for EMI lecturers and students, and the protocols for EMI lecturers and the dean or the academic director at the BIS universities.

The questionnaires and protocols were sent to three colleagues and a key researcher in the field of EMI, who provided feedback on the instruments.

The questionnaire for lecturers was a mix of open- and close-ended questions divided into four sections that aimed to investigate:

- Understanding about the use of EMI
- The existing Continuing Professional Development (CPD) opportunities for lecturers in the shift to EMI
- The extent to which EMI was actually being used in class
- The willingness of lecturers to participate in a case study

Regarding the questionnaire for students, it involved fifteen closed-ended questions, and a section for comments, that aimed to find out the extent to which lecturers use EMI in practice.

The questionnaires were sent to the gatekeepers at the participating BIS universities, who then shared the questionnaires with the EMI lecturers and students chosen by them.

Regarding the semi-structured interview protocols, they were not sent to lecturers or gatekeepers in this pilot phase. However, they were sent to the gatekeepers a few days before a case study was carried out. The purpose was to let the participants know the sort of questions that would be asked in the interviews.

The data collected from the pilot study involved thematic analysis.

The findings

The pilot project demonstrated that the research questions could indeed be answered, although at this stage the answers were limited because interviews with lecturers and the academic directors, document analysis, and class observations were planned to complete and complement the information gathered from the questionnaires.

In addition, it was noted that responses to research question 3 showed discrepancies that would be narrowed down after observing classes and interviewing lecturers.

Finally, initial findings showed that the lecturers were positive and open about teaching using EMI. They considered that the implementation of EMI has benefits for both students and lecturers. These benefits include the improvement of students and lecturers' English proficiency, as well as the possibility to obtain scholarships to study abroad. Also, according to the lecturers, the BIS universities provide them with a variety of opportunities to improve EMI, including workshops, formal and informal talks, and seminars.

In addition, some lecturers have had the opportunity to attend training courses in Canada and the USA. Furthermore, just over two-thirds of the lecturers say that they always pay attention to both language and content, consider the student's educational background and language proficiency when planning and teaching a technical subject, and provide students with information about learning strategies for both content and language. However, two-thirds do not evaluate the language; rather, they evaluate knowledge about subject content.

Finally, the lecturers feel that the BIS universities need to develop pre-service courses, courses that focus on pedagogy towards EMI, and take into account CPD opportunities.

References

Yin, R. (2009). *Case study research. Design and methods* (4th edition). Thousand Oaks, CA: SAGE Publications.

Yin, R. (2014). *Case study research. Design and methods* (5th edition). London: SAGE.

3 A case study

Introduction

English as a Medium of Instruction (EMI) in higher education (HE) is of global interest. Research has focused on the recruitment (Costa & Coleman, 2013) and the role of bilingual lecturers (Varghese, 2004). In addition, the evaluation of professional development programmes in bilingual settings (Zhang, 2014), at the different levels of evaluation (Guskey, 2002), have guided studies focused on the impact on pedagogy (Goodman, 2014), the effect of training (Klaassen & Graaff, 2001a), and lecturers' experiences and perspectives (Ai, 2016; Chapple, 2015; Unterberger & Wilhelmer, 2011; Werther et al., 2014).

Most of the recent research has been conducted in Europe, Asia, and Africa (Macaro, 2017) in non-English-speaking countries, such as Japan, China, Turkey, Italy, Australia, Spain, and France. In addition, a few research projects have been conducted in Latin America, in countries such as Brazil, Colombia, and Venezuela (Dearden, 2015). Unfortunately, no research has been conducted in Mexico, although this country has been implementing a BIS modality in its tertiary education programmes since 2012.

This summary, then, is the product of the first case study looking at EMI conducted in Mexico. The main aim of this research was to explore the implications on the CPD and training for lecturers in the current shift to EMI in BIS universities.

In addition, this case study pretends to add a Mexican dimension to both previous and ongoing research projects in other countries such as, amongst many others, Korea (Park, 2015), Ukraine (Goodman, 2014), Vietnam (Vu & Burns, 2014), and Egypt (El-Fiki, 2012).

Summary

Problem statement

English is becoming the lingua franca of the global community in education (Ishikawa, 2016); therefore, there is a growing demand for learning English and using EMI in many world contexts (El-Fiki, 2012). Thus, English language skills are seen as vital for the countries that want to have access to the information that forms the basis of social, educational, and economic development. Hence, particularly in non-English-speaking countries, learning and teaching are being re-evaluated, first through the introduction of professional development opportunities for lecturers (Burns & Richards, 2009 cited by El-Fiki, 2012). As such, research towards the improvement of EMI has been conducted to support initiatives, reforms, and development plans in countries such as Japan, Malaysia, the Maldives, Nepal, in Asia (Obaidul et al., 2013), and in Ukraine (Goodman, 2014, Denmark (Werther et al., 2014), and Egypt (El-Fiki, 2012), amongst other countries in Asia, Europe, and Africa.

In Mexico, decision-makers have embraced a top-down internationalization statement in their decision to implement BIS technological and polytechnic universities. However, unlike the countries mentioned previously, there is no clear information regarding initiatives or policies that evidence support for lecturers in making the shift to EMI. In addition, in Latin America, there is scarce research (Macaro, 2017) on the professional development of lecturers and how lecturers perceive, respond, and generally react to either the idea or, indeed, the implementation of EMI initiatives. Thus, problematizing the move towards EMI, exposing the limitations, as well as exploring the implications in the professional development of lecturers in the current EMI environment seemed to be a suitable approach to providing recommendations and/or solutions to an increasing number of issues that might have already arisen or could arise in the future.

The research questions

1 What are lecturer's existing thoughts, ideas, and beliefs about the use of EMI?
2 What are the existing continuing professional development and training opportunities provided to EMI lecturers?
3 How and to what extent are lecturers currently using EMI in their teaching?

4   How might the continuing professional development and training opportunities for lecturers be improved to more adequately meet their needs in implementing EMI?

Participants and participants' selection

The research involved the participation of EMI lecturers, students, and both the Dean, and the Academic Director of the Technological University El Retoño (the UTR).

First of all, the recruited participants consented to be observed and video recorded in class and interviewed. To this end, as was done in research studies such as Vu and Burns (2014), El-Fiki (2012), and Vinke et al. (1998), questionnaires were administered first. Information gathered from questionnaires provided with lecturers' characteristics and willingness to participate in class observation and interviews.

Then, I decided to select the participants who would take part in the whole research, using a purposive sampling technique. I identified lecturer's characteristics from data obtained in the questionnaires, and I chose the most relevant candidates for the class observation, which was followed by a stimulated recall and interview, based on the following criteria:

- Lecturers who were not English teachers
  From my English teaching experience, I have had the opportunity to see that English teachers usually have attended courses that focus on pedagogy to teach English as a second language. In this sense, I foresaw that those lecturers who have been English teachers would have an advantage (in pedagogy) to teach using EMI. Thus, I considered that selecting lecturers with less pedagogical experience in English teaching would provide a clearer view on the implications of using EMI to teach a technical subject.
- Lecturers that hold a minimum B2 English
  According to the Guidelines for the Implementation of the BIS Model (SES, 2014; see Appendix C), a lecturer who teaches his or her technical subject(s) in English at a TSU or engineering level should hold a B2 English language level. Thus, I foresaw that selecting a lecturer who fulfils this minimum requirement would let me see to what extent this English language level allowed the lecturer to teach his or her technical subject in English.
- Lecturers who are experienced in EMI and are currently teaching their subjects in English

Based on my experience, many higher education institutions hire lecturers every academic year. Then, I foresaw that there would be some lecturers who were just starting to teach at the BIS universities by the time I was conducting my research. Thus, it was relevant to have in mind that I was looking for lecturers who had experience teaching EMI for at least one year.

- Lecturers who learned English as a second language

  My research focuses on EMI lecturers in a non-English-speaking country. Thus, I decided not to select native English speakers because they would have advantages (on the use of the target language) over non-native speakers.

- Lecturers who have participated in training courses and/or professional development programmes provided by the participating BIS university

  I considered the possibility of finding a lecturer who had worked in another bilingual institution and he or she could have been trained to teach EMI there. If that was the case, his or her participation would not be relevant to answer my questions regarding the professional development opportunities provided by the participating BIS university.

- Lecturers who belong to one of the three main positions (or categories) distinguished by the Mexican Technological and Polytechnic Subsystem.

From my experience working in a technological university, depending on the position of the lecturer, he or she has more or less academic and administrative responsibilities. Thus, I considered it relevant to select lecturers who belong to each of the three positions (categories) because they might have different points of view regarding the training and professional development opportunities provided by the BIS institution, which would enrich my data. Table 3.1 displays further information regarding the positions distinguished by the Mexican Technological and Polytechnic Subsystem.

Finally, considering that I conducted research based on *sociocultural theory*, which allowed me to see how lecturers learn to teach EMI by constructing experiences with a variety of "members of the teaching profession" (Freeman & Johnson, 1998, p. 401), I foresaw that the single participation of lecturers would provide me with limited information regarding their professional development and pedagogical practices. Thus, in addition to lecturers, my participants included the Dean, Academic Director, and students whose participation complements answers to research question 2: *What are the existing professional development opportunities for lecturers in the shift to EMI?* and research question 4: *How might professional development opportunities for lecturers be improved to more adequately meet their needs in implementing EMI?*

Regarding the participation of the students, there was only one requirement. Those students who responded on the questionnaires would have been attending classes with those lecturers who were observed in class and interviewed.

A sociocultural stance

Interpretations of the Vygotskian sociocultural theory by Lantolf and Frawley in 1984 (Lantolf, 2006) have been the baseline for the use of the sociocultural theory in disciplines such as second-language teaching.

When the sociocultural theory is adopted to teacher's education, it emphasizes that "teaching is constructed through experiences in and with students, parents, and administrators as well as other members of the teaching profession" (Freeman & Johnson, 1998, pp. 401, 402). Thus, the participation of the EMI lecturers, the Dean, the Academic Director and students was valuable from the sociocultural stance, which allows the participation of a number of stakeholders and, therefore, a variety of research methods that permit the triangulation of data towards answering the research questions.

Table 3.1 Positions or categories distinguished by the Mexican Technological Subsystem

Position (category) 1	Position (category) 2	Position (category) 3
Tutor (PTC) This is the full-time lecturer with the highest position and responsibilities. Usually, the tutors are the lecturers with more years of experience at the technological or polytechnic subsystem.	Technician lecturer (TD) This is a full-time lecturer. Although TD professional experience is similar to that of the tutors, a TD has fewer responsibilities, and usually has less experience at the technological or polytechnic subsystem.	Unit lecturer (PA) This lecturer works ten to thirty hours a week. PAs are, usually, those with less experience. Most of them get contracts per term.

Note: The three different positions are related to the lecturer's academic activities as well as responsibilities, and professional experience in the academic and industrial sectors.

Source: This table was developed by the author for the purpose of the book, based on her experience and knowledge on the technological subsystem.

Validity and reliability

"Case studies have to abide by canons of validity and reliability" (Cohen et al., 2011, p. 295). Within qualitative studies it means "accuracy of the findings and documentation of as many steps of the procedures as possible" (Creswell, 2009, p. 190; Yin, 2003, cited by Creswell, 2009). Thus, to provide validity and reliability for this study, I triangulated different data sources, and used a rich and a thick description of the setting. In addition, I presented "negative or discrepant information" and spent a prolonged time in the field, as suggested by Gibbs (2007, cited by Creswell, 2009). I did this by first using a variety of data sources to examine evidence and provide a coherent justification of the findings. In addition, I compared interview data with classroom observation data and documented all discrepancies or information that was not compatible with themes that emerged during analysis. Furthermore, I provided a solid contextual description of the findings (see Chapter 4). Finally, I have maintained communication with the participants (gatekeepers) during and after the period of the study, as suggested by Yin (2014) and Cohen et al. (2011).

Ethical considerations

By the time I conducted this case study, I was registered as a PhD student at the University of Bristol. Thus, this research was undertaken within a structured framework which included the institutional procedures, as suggested in the Graduate School of Education's (GSoE) ethics procedures (2016). In addition, I followed the principles (respect, value, social responsibility, and minimizing harm) suggested by the ethics guidelines for Internet-mediated research, published by The British Psychological Society (2013).

This research started by contacting the institutional gatekeepers (Seidman, 2006), on May 2017, at the BIS universities chosen (described in Chapter 1) to negotiate access for both a pilot and a research to the researcher. Once the access was granted, potential participants were contacted via e-mail. A formal letter was attached to the e-mail in order to approach the potential participants in a professional way. Sufficient information (Polit & Tatano, 2004) regarding the purpose of the study was provided to the participants.

There were also some risks regarding confidentiality and anonymity (Tashakkori & Teddlie, 2009). In order to avoid these risks, names or addresses or any other identifiable characteristics were not required.

Data collection and research methods

For this research, data were gathered between June and August 2017 through online surveys for EMI lecturers and students, semi-structured interviews (carried out with EMI lecturers and the Dean and Academic Director at the UTR), structured and semi-structured classroom observations, stimulated recalls, focus groups with lecturers, and documentary sources.

EMI lecturers responded to a mix of open- and close-ended questions in an online survey. The questionnaire was developed in four sections (lecturer's thoughts about the use of EMI, the current CPD opportunities to EMI lecturers, usage of EMI, and the improvement on the CPD of EMI lecturers) with a total of twenty questions. Students' survey involved fifteen questions related to the usage of EMI in the classroom by their EMI teacher.

Regarding the structured observation, the Sheltered Instruction Observation Protocol (SIOP) Model (The Centre for Applied Linguistics, 2017) was adopted and adapted to fulfil the research needs, as done by Park (2015). The unstructured class observation, on the other side, involved taking notes of what was observed in the classroom, along with interpretations about the systems, settings, and people's behaviours (O'Leary, 2014).

The lecturers selected were observed using EMI in a one-hour class teaching a variety of subjects such as Planning and Organization of Work, Statistics for Business, Customer Studies, Applied Differential Equations, Visual Programming, Integration of Automatic System, Local Area Networks, and the Dynamics of Machines.

Data analysis

Thematic analysis and descriptive statistics were used to describe and summarize all data collected in this exploratory case study. Thematic analysis allowed me to use a qualitative analysis method to communicate the observations, findings, and interpretations and understanding within the research context (Boyatzis, 1998). A brief summary of the data analysis is provided by research method in the following paragraphs.

- Online surveys to EMI lecturers
    Thirty-four EMI lecturers responded to a survey—twenty-two males and twelve females. All the lecturers were Mexican—thirty-one unit lecturers, and three technician lecturers with a variety

of profiles—mechatronics, business, technologies for information and communication, human resources, English language teaching, software development, and visual effects and animation. Lecturers responded to a mix of open- and close-ended questions developed in google forms.[1]

- Classroom observations

    Eight out of thirty-four EMI lecturers, six men and two women, were selected to participate in structured and unstructured classroom observations.

- Stimulated recall sessions

    Eight lecturers participated in stimulated recall sessions (Klaassen & Graaff, 2001b), six men and two women. The video recorded class was provided to the lecturers who were asked to watch themselves (individually) teaching their class in English and reflect on their teaching methods and their needs to improve their EMI teaching.

- Focus group

    Four EMI lecturers participated in a focus group (three men and one woman), and two (one man and one woman) were individually interviewed. Unfortunately, for this phase of the research, two lecturers (two men) did not have the opportunity to participate. One of them couldn't attend due to unexpected activities, and the other lecturer simply did not arrive to either of the two options provided to him—the focus group or the individual interview.

- Online surveys to students

    As many as 122 students whose teachers were observed and interviewed were asked to answer an online survey—65 men, 54 women, 1 "other," and 2 who preferred not to say. Almost all the students were Mexican (121), and there was 1 American, all again from a variety of academic backgrounds.

- Semi-structured interview: Administrative staff

    The Dean and the Academic Director were also interviewed. The semi-structured interview was focused on the CPD provided to the EMI lecturers. However, there was also an opportunity to discuss about the BIS modality in an unstructured interview.

- Documents

    Documents accessed online were the General Guidelines for the Implementation of BIS Model (see Appendix C) and the Blue Book.

Regarding the information provided by the Academic Director from the UTR, it involved a number of documents, including the guidelines for recruitment, selection, and induction of personnel to the BIS modality,[2] a document being developed[3] by the UTR that aims to include in the BIS modality in the Blue Book, training programmes brochures offered by a variety of international institutions, observation protocols for class and laboratory sessions, a checklist for the implementation of the BIS modality, and a PowerPoint presentation, that discusses on the facilities offered to students, the academic modality, as well as the variety of cultural activities performed by the students at the UTR. It also provides details of the international partner groups that are part of the BIS modality; these groups include the English language fellow, the teacher mobility programme, and Peace Corps Mexico (further information on these groups and their main activities are discussed in Chapter 4).

Notes

1 The rationale to have used Google Forms for this research lies in the boundaries that it offers. With this freely available online tool, it is possible to create and analyse surveys in the web browser. In addition, no especial software is required.
2 This document displays a flowchart and provides a description of the recruitment and selection process of lecturers at the UTR.
3 A draft document that was to be provided to the CGUTyP by the end of 2017, so that this information was included in the updated version of the Blue Book.

References

Ai, B. (2016). Becoming a bilingual teacher in a Chinese university: A case study. *Reflective Practice, 17*(5), 605–620. doi:10.1080/14623943.2016.1184637.

Boyatzis, R. (1998). *Transforming qualitative information: Thematic analysis and code development*. Thousand Oaks, CA: SAGE.

Burns, A., & Richards, J. (Eds.). (2009). *The Cambridge guide to second language teacher education*. Cambridge: Cambridge University Press.

Chapple, J. (2015). Teaching in English is not necessarily the teaching of English. *International Education Studies, 8*(3), 1–13.

Cohen, L., Manion, L., & Morrison, K. (2011). *Research methods in education*. London: Routledge.

Costa, F., & Coleman, J. (2013). A survey of English-medium instruction in Italian higher education. *International Journal of Bilingual Education and Bilingualism, 16*(1), 3–19. doi:10.1080/13670050.2012.676621.

Creswell, J. (2009). *Research design: Qualitative, quantitative, and mixed methods approach* (3rd edition). London: SAGE.

Dearden, J. (2015). English as a medium of instruction—A growing global phenomenon. British Council. Report 2014/E484. Retrieved 20 January

2017, from https://www.britishcouncil.org/education/ihe/knowledge-centre/english-language-higher-education/report-english-medium-instruction.

El-Fiki, H. (2012). Teaching English as a foreign language and using English as a medium of instruction in Egypt: Teachers' perceptions of teaching approaches and sources of change. Doctoral thesis, University of Toronto.

Freeman, D., & Johnson, K. E. (1998). Reconceptualizing the knowledge-base of language teacher education. *TESOL Quarterly, 32*(3), 397–417.

Gibbs, G. R. (2007). Analysing qualitative data. In U. Flick (Ed.), *The SAGE qualitative research kit*. London: SAGE.

Goodman, B. (2014). Implementing English as a medium of instruction in a Ukrainian University: Challenges, adjustments, and opportunities. *International Journal of Pedagogies and Learning, 9*(2), 130–141.

GSoE Ethics procedures. (n.d.). Retrieved 20 November 2016, from http://www.bristol.ac.uk/education/research/networks/ethicscommittee/procedures/.

Guskey, T. (2002). *Evaluating professional development*. Thousand Oaks, CA: SAGE.

Ishikawa, T. (2016). World Englishes and English as a Lingua Franca: Conceptualising the legitimacy of Asian people's English. *Asian Englishes, 18*(2), 129–140. doi:10.1080/13488678.2016.1171672.

Klaassen, R., & De Graaff, E. (2001a). Facing innovation: Preparing lecturers for English-medium instruction in a non-native context. *European Journal of Engineering Education, 26*(3), 281–289.

Klaasseen, R., & De Graff, E. (2001b). The international university curriculum: Challenges in English-medium engineering education. Doctoral thesis, Technische Universiteit Delft.

Lantolf, J. (2006). Sociocultural theory and L2: State of the art. *Studies in Second Language Acquisition, 28*(1), 67–109. doi:10.1017/S0272263106060037.

Macaro, E. (2017). Systematic review of English medium instruction. University of Oxford podcast. Audio and video lectures. *EMI Oxford Symposium*, 22 June. Retrieved 13 July 2017, from http://podcasts.ox.ac.uk/systematic-review-english-medium-instruction.

Obaidul, M., Mai, H. T., & Baldauf, R. (2013). Medium of instruction in Asia: Context, processes and outcomes. *Current Issues in Language Planning, 14*(1), 1–15.

O'Leary, M. (2014). *Classroom observation. A guide to the effective observation of teaching and learning*. London: Routledge.

Park, J. (2015). Pedagogical knowledge and needs for professional development and support for English medium instruction of university professors. Doctoral thesis, Indiana University.

Polit, D., & Tatano, C. (2004). *Nursing research: Principles and methods* (7th edition). London: Lippincott Williams and Wilkins.

Seidman, I. (2006). *Interviewing as qualitative research: A guide for researchers in education and the social sciences* (3rd edition). New York and London: Teacher's College, Columbia University.

SES. (2014). Guidelines for the implementation of the BIS model in technological and polytechnic universities. Retrieved 10 May 2017, from https://www.gob.mx/busqueda.

Tashakkori, A., & Teddlie, C. (2009). *Foundations of mixed methods in social and behavioral sciences*. Thousand Oaks, CA: SAGE.
The British Psychological Society. (2013). Retrieved 20 November 2016, from http://www.bps.org.uk/system/files/Public%20files/inf206-guidelines-for-internet-mediated-research.pdf.
The Centre for Applied Linguistics. (2017). SIOP – Home. Retrieved 14 February 2017, from http://www.cal.org/siop/.
Unterberger, B., & Wilhelmer, N. (2011). English-medium education in economics and business studies. *ITL – International Journal of Applied Linguistics, 161*, 90–110. doi:10.1075/itl.161.06unt.
Varghese, M. (2004). Professional development for bilingual teachers in the United States: A Site for articulating and contesting professional roles. *International Journal of Bilingual Education and Bilingualism, 7*(2–3), 222–237.
Villegas-Reimers, E. (2003). *Teacher professional development: An international review of the literature.* Paris: UNESCO International Institute for Educational Planning.
Vinke, A. A., Snippe, J., & Jochems, W. (1998). English-medium content courses in Non-English higher education: A study of lecturer experiences and teaching behaviours. *Teaching in Higher Education, 3*(3), 383–394. doi:10.1080/1356215980030307.
Vu, N., & Burns, A. (2014). English as a medium of instruction: Challenges for Vietnamese tertiary lecturers. *The Journal of Asia TEFL, 11*(3), 1–31.
Werther, C., Denver, L., Jensen, C., & Mees, I. (2014). Using English as a medium of instruction at university level in Denmark: The lecturer's perspective. *Journal of Multilingual and Multicultural Development, 35*(5), 443–462.
Yin, R. (2003). *Case study research. Design and methods* (3rd edition). London: SAGE.
Yin, R. (2014). *Case study research. Design and methods* (5th edition). London: SAGE.
Zhang, Y. (2014). Investigating the impact of a university-based professional development program for teachers of English language learners in Ohio—A mixed methods study of teacher learning and change. Master thesis, Ohio State University.

4 The findings

Participant's personal and professional characteristics

As discussed in previous chapters, this is the first time that a research on EMI in BIS universities is conducted. Thus, it was relevant to present the participants' personal (age, gender, nationality, etc.), and professional information (discipline, position at the technological/polytechnic subsystem, and English language background and proficiency, experience teaching EMI, etc.).

First of all, by the time this research was conducted, the teaching staff at the UTR involved fifty lecturers from a variety of disciplines, thirty-four (70% of the current staff) of them answered the online questionnaire, and 64.7% of the lecturers are men and 35.3% are women.

The participants' age ranged between 21 and 60 years. The age range between 21 and 30 years represents 47.1% of the respondents, and 29.4% represents those aged between 41 and 50 years. The remaining 17.7% and 8.8% represent ages between 31 and 40 years and 51 and 60 years, respectively.

In relation to EMI lecturers' position at the UTR, 91.2% of them are unit lecturers, while the remaining 8.8% are full-time lecturers.

With regard to lecturers' professional profile, the information is diverse. Profiles related to mechatronics lead with a 23.5%. Then the profiles on business and technologies and information and communication accounted for 17.6% each. Profiles related to human resources and English language teaching constituted 11.8% each. Other profiles such as education, industrial engineering, and human development accounted for 8.8% of the lecturer's profiles. Finally, profiles related to software development and visual effects and animation constituted 5.9% and 2.9% of the sample, respectively.

With respect to the nationality, 100% of the participants said they are Mexican. However, just 97.1% of the lecturers considered Spanish

The findings 33

as their first language. The remaining 2.9% considered English as their first language.

Regarding the participants' English language background, 79.4% of the lecturers said that they learnt English attending specific English language courses, 65.7% learnt English at private schools, 50% at public schools, and 2.9% of the participants said that they learnt English by either studying in the USA, being an autodidact (using the Internet and other sources), working at an international company, or taking part in exchange programmes in the USA.

In regard to lecturers' English language level, it varies between A2 and C2. Then, 2.9% of the participants hold an A2 level, 5.9% hold B1, 38.2% B2, 29.4% C1, and 11.8% C2. As much as 11.8% say that they do not know of their proficiency level in English.

About teaching using EMI 44.1% of the lecturers have 0–1 years of experience, 14.7% 1–2, 14.7% 2–3, 8.8% 3–4, and 11.8% 4–5. As much as 2.95% of the participants said that they have taught using EMI for more than ten years. The rest, 2.95%, did not provide an answer in this respect.

As discussed in Chapter 1, the UTR provides two academic levels: TSU and engineering. In relation to these academic levels, 59.1% of the lecturers said that they teach at both levels, 36.4% teach at the TSU level, and 4.5% teach at the engineering level. The academics also said that they teach a variety of subjects using EMI at these TSU and engineering levels, these being accounting, finance, analogue and digital electronics, business administration, computer-aided manufacturing, database, human development, management, instrumentation, language arts, learning and evaluation, marketing, microcontrollers, networking, pneumatic and hydraulic systems, programming, business informatics, software, web application development, statistics for business, teaching strategies, and teaching productive and receptive skills.

Finally, considering that being an English language teacher would be extremely relevant for the selection of the participants in class observation and interviews (discussion on this topic is provided in Chapter 3), it was extremely important to gather information in this regard. Then, 64.7% of the participants said that they have never been English language teachers. The remaining 35.3% said that they have been involved in English language teaching at public and private institutions in basic, secondary, and tertiary education, including teaching English at the UTR.

Having analysed and presented the characteristics of the EMI lecturers at the participating BIS university, the following steps are used to present the findings. These are reported in four sections related to the research questions:

1. Lecturer's existing thoughts, ideas, and beliefs of the use of EMI
2. The existing professional development opportunities provided by the BIS university to EMI lecturers
3. The manner and extent to which lecturers are currently using EMI within their class
4. How might continuing professional development opportunities for EMI lecturers be improved

Lecturer's existing thoughts, ideas, and beliefs about the use of EMI

Research question 1 was basically answered with information gathered from the questionnaire administrated and interviews with EMI lecturers.

Almost 80% of the EMI lecturers thought that the use of EMI in HE settings is a new approach to teach their subjects and an opportunity for students to learn both English and content. About 60% of the participants said that EMI is a new approach to teach their subjects and also an opportunity for themselves to practice and hone their English language proficiency. Just short of 20% of the lecturers thought that EMI is a new approach/method to teach English. Just over 20% of the participants consider that it is a new approach to learn English.

In addition, all the participants thought that teaching their subjects in English is beneficial for both students and lecturers. According to the respondents, the improvement in students' English level can later translate into better job opportunities, internships in the global industries, and the possibility to obtain scholarships abroad.

Participants also consider that lecturers can benefit by becoming stronger candidates when applying for scholarships because their English proficiency improves when teaching using EMI.

Finally, more or less all the lecturers (99.4%) displayed a positive attitude towards the use of EMI in tertiary education with 92.2% claiming to be open to and very interested in learning how to teach using EMI.

However, about 65% of the lecturers considered EMI challenging and sometimes difficult, and just short of 10% thought that EMI is not only time consuming but also not necessarily the best way for students to improve either their English or, indeed, to learn content.

Existing professional development opportunities for lecturers provided by the BIS university

The answer to research question 2 involved the collection of data related to lecturers' training and professional development opportunities offered by the UTR. Therefore, the study needed to gather information from all possible sources, these being documents open to public access online, and documents provided by the UTR, interviews with the Dean and the Academic Director, and a set of questions developed and included in the survey for the EMI lecturers.

Then, according to EMI lecturers:

- 47% have been involved in training courses.
- 41% have participated in informal talks.
- 32% have attended formal talks.
- 27% have participated in workshops.
- 3% have attended seminars.

In addition, since 2013 the UTR has offered a number of national, local (within the UTR), and international training opportunities (Appendix E displays the training opportunities offered by the UTR since 2013 and the participants in a variety of programmes).

The national training opportunities include programmes that support the EMI teaching staff in one way or another, and all lecturers have to take the courses. The different training courses are listed as follows:

- **Induction course:** developed to provide lecturers with basic information about the technological universities, the competencies model, and the BIS modality.
- **English Skills Reinforcement (ERC):** aims to teach English to EMI lecturers in order to improve and reinforce their English language skills. This course is delivered by the UTR English Language Department.
- **The English Language Fellow:** this programme is in collaboration with personnel at the U.S. Embassy who provide experienced English teachers to assist with the development and improvement of the BIS modality at the UTR.
- **Technical English:** was implemented to teach technical English to EMI lecturers and English language teachers. The course is taught by English Language Fellows from the USA.

36 The findings

- **Pedagogy:** the UTR has developed courses that focus on didactic sequence planning, teaching, assessment, and learning evidence retrieved in order to develop lecturers' pedagogical skills.
- **Micro teaching:** a course developed to teach lecturers how to manage volume of their voice, how to walk around the class, and how to elicit information from students.
- **Replication course:** UTR lecturers who have taken training courses abroad replicate the course(s) to those lecturers who have not had the opportunity to travel. The replication course(s) are usually developed online and have to include an evaluation phase.
- **The teacher mobility programme:** the SEP provides teacher assistants from both the USA and France.
- **Peace Corps Mexico:** a volunteer comes to the UTR to promote world peace and help with language training and teaching.

Finally, in addition to the aforementioned courses, the UTR has developed strategies towards the use of technical vocabulary as well as instruments to both evaluate and decide the most appropriate training needs to EMI lecturers, these being:

- **Glossary of technical terms:** provides EMI lecturers with a list of technical terms that aim at establishing a standardized use of technical jargon amongst classes.
- **Class observation and laboratory observation forms:** the UTR has developed two instruments for observation. The aim of these instruments is to evaluate an EMI lecturer teaching a regular class or a class in a laboratory (also called a practical class). Then, based on the observation, the observer, who is part of the administrative staff, decides the kind of training that best-suits the EMI lecturers' needs. The two observation forms have similar characteristics. They have been developed to evaluate the use of English language, class planning, the introduction to the topic, development of the class, and class closing. The forms include a section to provide feedback to the lecturer. However, unexpectedly, the observation forms are in Spanish.
- **International training:** international opportunities, on the other hand, are supported by international partner groups or allies that offer a variety of mobility programmes. The UTR reported 377 international opportunities in its first five years (2013–2017). Interestingly, the international opportunities have been open to EMI lecturers, English teachers, students, and administrative staff. However, for this research only those international opportunities focused on EMI lecturers were presented.

As stated previously, EMI lecturers then, have open access to international opportunities. However, the UTR has structured a selection process. The selection process involves five filters:

1   Time spent working at the UTR. The lecturer should have worked at the UTR for at least two terms. However, there are cases where the lecturer has worked only for one term.
2   Teaching evaluation outcomes.
3   English proficiency. The lecturers should hold a B2 English language level and should prove it by presenting a certificate or diploma.
4   The Academic Coordinator's approval.
5   The administrative performance of the lecturer.

Once the EMI lecturers are selected, they have the opportunity to attend one of the next available programmes:

- **Content Area Teacher Training (CATT):** The Georgian College, Canada

This is a 100-hour course that aims to develop reading and comprehension skills, and knowledge exchange between lecturers who teach technical subjects in English. This course also includes class observation (and evaluation) related to the subject taught by the lecturer.

- **Content Area Teacher Training (CATT):** Center for English as a Second Language (CESL) at the University of Arizona, USA

This is a 120-hour course that focuses on pedagogical needs of trainees to address ways to scaffold English materials designed and written for native speakers and to address the linguistic needs of the trainees.

In addition to the current international mobility programmes, the UTR claims to be looking ahead towards the improvement of CPD and training of EMI lecturers. Thus, the UTR, together with its alliances in Canada, have been developing a 140-hour training programme and certification proposal. The programme is planned to be delivered in a blended format, including pre- and post-work, to take place in Mexico and face-to-face instruction in Canada at Georgian College, in the city of Barrie, Ontario. The training programme would address, among other things:

a   Strategies to help students process textbook information
b   Note-taking strategies to focus students' attention and guide learning

c   Helping students with studying and test-taking
d   Good practices in online learning.

According to the Academic Director, it is planned to provide an additional session on designing meaningful assignments.

The manner and extent to which lecturers are currently using EMI within their class

The evidence suggests that the lecturers use EMI before, during, and after the class. These three periods, pre-, during- and post-class, involve a series of activities planned, carried out, and reviewed by the lecturers.

Pre-class: the pre-class period comprises class preparation. Almost 75% of the lecturers pay attention to both content and language objectives of the lesson preparation and their fit with the educational background and language proficiency of the students. Explicit links between ideas and students' backgrounds are also considered to be part of this period.

During the class: this refers basically to four main activities done within the class:

a   Activities and materials that lecturers employ to make content accessible to students with limited language proficiency
b   Providing learners with information about learning strategies
c   Opportunities for interaction and discussion
d   the adequacy of hands-on material so that students have the opportunity to apply content and language knowledge

Regarding activities and materials, most of the lecturers use a variety of strategies in English or a combination of English and Spanish, almost 25% of the lecturers translate to Spanish when needed, and just a few of the lecturers use a variety of strategies completely in Spanish. In addition, most of the lecturers use easy, practical examples, synonyms, and provision of glossaries to make content more accessible. Nevertheless, the majority of lecturers would allow the use of Spanish if understanding and learning might be at risk. Lecturers do let students ask questions in Spanish but respond in English with easier examples. Finally, some lecturers prefer to provide students with material (readings and PowerPoint slides) beforehand and use materials in Spanish.

In relation to learning strategies, more than 50% of the lecturers offer students a variety of learning strategies towards both language learning and content, about 25% consider only content, and a few lecturers never provide students with learning strategies. However, during the interviews the lecturers mentioned that more than learning strategies as such, they provide students with learning tips, such as the use of websites, reading specific books in English or Spanish, and writing down new ideas and examples in their own (i.e. the students' own words).

As for opportunities for interaction and discussion, almost all the lecturers provide them by dividing students into smaller groups or teams focusing on specific topics for discussion or conducting practical activities within a workshop or laboratory. However, a few lecturers consider providing students with opportunities to interact and "talk" is just a way to let students speak in their mother tongue. These few lecturers prefer not to let the students interact too much with each other. This last claim is similar to responses provided by a few students.

Regarding the adequacy of hands-on material, almost all the lecturers provide adequate or better hands-on materials. However, a few do not, and this matches with comments provided by a few students.

The post-class period: this has to do with the review of concepts and vocabulary; assessment of students' learning; evaluation of content, language, or a combination of both; and the provision of feedback.

First of all, almost all the lecturers have developed a process that includes a review of the concepts (in English) at the end of each term. In addition, this review does not take into account vocabulary, the focus being content rather than language.

Regarding the assessment of students' learning, more than 67% of the lecturers assess in English, almost 33% do the assessment process combining English and Spanish, and just a few lecturers assess students in Spanish.

In relation to the evaluation of content, more than 50% of the lecturers evaluate a combination of the content and the English language. Almost 33% of the lecturers evaluate the knowledge of the technical subject taught, and, a small number, about 8%, evaluate the English language developed and vocabulary acquired.

With reference to feedback, more than 50% of the lecturers provide feedback using a combination of English and Spanish after written exams and projects. About 25% of the lecturers provide immediate feedback in the class in English after oral presentations or when the whole class seems to have doubts about concepts, ideas, and the like. In addition, a few lecturers use Spanish when providing one-to-one feedback after class. Finally, when providing feedback to students, 67% of the lecturers focus on both the content and the improvement of the English language. Almost 33% of the lecturers focus only on the technical subject, and a few lecturers focus mainly on the English language.

How might professional development opportunities for EMI lecturers be improved

Although a few lecturers said there is no need to improve the current CPD and training opportunities provided by the BIS university, the majority of the lecturers believe that improvements are possible, these being:

- Courses focused on pedagogy
- Teaching EMI
- Teaching to students with low English language proficiency
- Students' learning
- Assessment and feedback
- The use of technology to teach EMI
- Technical English for lecturers relative to their major as well as general English to improve lecturers' English language proficiency
- Pre-service and in-service courses regarding the use of EMI
- Class observation and feedback from peers who teach the same subject or teach in the same area; it would also be necessary to get feedback from native speakers
- EMI certification
- Lecturers' suggestions to improve the CPD programme
- Lecturers' general and specific needs
- Access to electronic libraries where original sources of information are in English

Finally, a few lecturers claim that they need help with students' English proficiency because they consider that it is not possible to teach, for example, advanced calculus at a C2 level to an A2 or B1 student. Also, regarding students, lecturers thought that English for specific purposes rather than general English should be taught in regular English classes. Lecturers consider that learning a subject in English is also the students' responsibility (as well as the lecturers and significant others) and that the university should work towards making this very clear to the students—that they (the students) are, at the end of the day, responsible for their own learning. Finally, one lecturer claimed that it is not possible to teach, for instance, Mexican labour law completely in English.

The students further highlighted and concurred with the lecturers' comments regarding training and CPD opportunities, in particular:

- Lecturers need to improve their classes generally, be more understanding, and demonstrate more interest in students' learning needs vis-à-vis content and language.
- Lecturers should be more helpful and should not only limit themselves to content—in a bilingual context, content and language go together.
- Checking pronunciation should be part of the class in their technical subjects.
- Lecturers should be open to use other resources (any new technology for instance) because the use of only PowerPoint presentations can be boring.
- Lecturers should be open to the use of Spanish from time to time to make content clearer to students.

5 Discussion, recommendations, and further research

Discussion and recommendations

The conclusions and recommendations are focused on three broad areas:

1 The general position and perception about using English as a medium of instruction (EMI)
2 Improvement of CPD and training programmes
3 EMI in practice

Regarding the general position and perception of EMI, the majority of the lecturers are positive, open, and eager to learn how to better deal with EMI. However, there are a few lecturers who are not fully convinced that EMI is necessarily the best way to provide bilingual education to a low-income population that needs to both develop language skills and improve content knowledge in order to be competitive in a globalized market. Thus, there is a need to clarify definitions and policy regarding EMI at BIS universities.

With respect to the variety of national, local, and international training provided to the lecturers since 2013, it is strong and positive towards developing better pedagogical practices, as well as for the improvement of lecturers' English language proficiency in both general and technical subjects. Nevertheless, the training has reached less than half of the current teaching staff, and, according to the Academic Director, the UTR has not developed a channel to receive recommendations from the lecturers. Regarding the effectiveness of training courses abroad, the UTR has not developed an instrument to evaluate them. In addition, to date, none of the courses provided have focused on the use of EMI, how to develop better EMI practices, when and how to use EMI, or to what extent EMI should be used. Last, the UTR has been able to design training courses to support lecturers CPD, in general; however, there is still a need to develop a more robust CPD programme that considers both pre- and in-service courses that ideally consider:

- An introduction to approaches to teaching in English.
- Teaching EMI in higher education.
- Use of first language in EMI contexts.
- Resources to teach EMI, the use of online platforms, and so on.
- Pedagogy.
- Students' learning.
- Class planning, assessment, and providing feedback, in EMI contexts.
- Evaluation of the CPD and training programmes periodically.
- The option to consider the development of a national certification for EMI lecturers, as done in other countries such as Denmark, in the University of Copenhagen; Germany, in the University of Freiburg; and Spain, in the Autonomous University of Madrid.
- The opportunity to share resources and experiences with national and/or international peers through either conferences or online platforms for EMI lecturers as for example in the course certification "EMI for academics" offered by the University of Southampton at Future Learn.

In addition, there are two areas that need addressing simultaneously in relation to the foregoing suggestions:

a   Provide access to online libraries and journals to both lecturers and students, and
b   Consider introducing technical English into students' EFL classes.

With regard to the use of EMI in practice, there is a need to consider and implement common practices when planning a class, teaching, providing feedback, reviewing, and assessing. Mainly, there are four questions to be discussed and answered:

- Should class planning consider both content and language?
- Should lecturers, within the class, let students discuss in English or in their mother tongue?
- Should the review of concepts be done in English or Spanish?
- Should feedback and assessment be in English or Spanish or a combination of both?

In these matters, the UTR could perhaps consider gathering EMI lecturers together to discuss these points and determine the best way forward for lecturers, students, and the university.

Further research

As previously mentioned, this is the first research conducted in Mexico since the introduction of the BIS model back in 2012. At the time the present research was conducted, that is, in 2017, there were twenty-one universities (amongst technological and polytechnic universities) working under a BIS modality, which implies the use of EMI. By September 2018, it was expected that thirty-one BIS universities would be implementing the use of EMI. Indeed, this implementation occurred. By the time this book was finished, there were twenty-nine BIS universities—nineteen technological and ten polytechnic. Thus, it is clear that there is a need to conduct further research that explores the implications of EMI for both teaching and learning. Therefore, it is necessary for researchers and stakeholders to put Mexico onto the EMI research map directly as well as making more use of research findings to both improve practice and to make recommendations for further developments.

Furthermore, the hope is that the results of this study will provide an insight and understanding about the state of EMI in Mexico. In addition, this study will open the door for more research. In this sense, the present study fulfils the need to research local initiatives regarding EMI, as suggested by Wilkinson (2013). However, the most valuable contribution of this study is the research itself because this study is the first of its kind to be conducted focusing on EMI at BIS universities in Mexico and specifically EMI's impact on tertiary education in Mexico, a country and an education system that are to date being ignored.

Reference

Wilkinson, R. (2013) English-medium instruction at a Dutch university: Challenges and pitfalls. In A. Doiz, D. Lasagabaster, & J. M. Sierra (Eds.), *English-medium instructions at universities global challenges*. Bristol: Multilingual Matters.

Appendix A
Current BIS technological and polytechnic universities spread in Mexico

Technological BIS universities established in 2012–2016	Polytechnic BIS universities established in 2012–2016
1. Technological University of El Retoño Borned BIS 2012; http://www.utr.edu.mx/www/index.php/es/	1. Polytechnic University of Santa Rosa Jauregui BIS, since 2013; http://upsrj.edu.mx/
2. Technological University of Chihuahua BIS, since 2013; http://www.utch.edu.mx/bis.html	2. Polytechnic University of Cuautitlán Izcalli BIS, since 2013; http://upci.edu.mx/
3. Technological University of Laja Bajío BIS, since 2013; http://www.utlbcelaya.com/	3. Polytechnic University Metropolitan of Hidalgo BIS, since 2014; http://upmetropolitana.edu.mx/
4. Technological University of Saltillo BIS, since 2013; http://utsaltillo.edu.mx/	4. Polytechnic University of Monclova-Frontera BIS, since 2015; http://upmf.edu.mx/
5. Technological University of San Luis Río Colorado BIS, since 2013; https://www.utslrc.edu.mx/	5. Polytechnic University Metropolitan of Puebla BIS, since 2016; http://www.metropoli.edu.mx/
6. Technological University of Metropolitan of Valle de México BIS, since 2013; http://utvam.edu.mx/	6. Polytechnic University of Yucatan Borned BIS in 2016; http://www.upy.edu.mx
7. Technological University of General Mariano Escobedo BIS, since 2014; http://www.ute.edu.mx/	7. Polytechnic University of Ramos Arizpe; BIS since 2016 http://upra.mx/
8. Technological University of Durango BIS, since 2015; http://www.utd.edu.mx/campus_bis/index.php	

(Continued)

9. Technological University of Laguna
BIS, since 2015; http://www.utlaguna.edu.mx/
10. Technological University of Mineral de la Reforma
BIS, since 2015; http://www.utmirbis.org/
11. Technological University of Guaymas
BIS, since 2016; http://www.utguaymas.edu.mx/utg/
12. Technological University of Puebla
BIS, since 2016; www.utbispuebla.com.mx
13. Technological University of La Riviera Maya
BIS, since 2016; http://www.utrivieramaya.edu.mx/
14. Technological University of Gutierrez Zamora
BIS, since 2016; http://www.utgz.edu.mx/

Technological BIS universities established in 2017

15. Technological University of Acuña; http://utca.mx/
16. Technological University Metropolitan of Guadalajara; http://utzmg.edu.mx/home/
17. Technological University of Campeche; http://utcam.edu.mx/
18. Technological University Metropolitan of San Luis Potosí; https://utmslp.edu.mx/

Technological BIS universities established in 2018

19. Technological University of Zinacantepec; http://utzinacantepec.edomex.gob.mx/

Polytechnic BIS universities established in 2018

8. Polytechnic University Metropolitan of Aguascalientes; https://www.facebook.com/UTMABiS/
9. Polytechnic University of Texcoco; http://uptexcoco.edomex.gob.mx/
10. Polytechnic University of Otozolotepec; http://upotec.edomex.gob.mx/inicio

---

Initial information presented on the table was obtained from the official webpage of the UTR http://www.utr.edu.mx/www/index.php/es/about-us/modelo-educativo, and the CGUTyP http://cgut.sep.gob.mx/mapa/2015/mapa2016.php. Then, the information was complemented with a search conducted by the author, to identify the current twenty-nine BIS universities spread in Mexico, for the purpose of this book.

Appendix B
English language proficiency considered by the CEFR in its 2001 volume

English levels		Description of the language proficiency levels
Advance	C2	• Understands almost all he or she hears or reads. • Summarizes and restructures spoken and written information from a variety of sources. • Expresses himself or herself fluently, naturally, and accurately, in both simple and complex situations.
	C1	• Understands a great variety of exacting text and infers meaning. • Expresses fluently in a natural and sudden way. • Uses the language in a flexible and effective way for a variety of purposes, including social, academic, and professional. • Produces clear, detailed text on exacting subjects and demonstrates the use of patterns and connectors to organize his or her ideas.
Intermediate	B2	• Understands the most important ideas in complex texts, in concrete and abstract subjects, consisting of specialized discussions in his or her professional field. • Can interact with a degree of fluency and spontaneity that makes regular interaction with native speakers quite possible without strain for either party. • Produces clear, detailed text on a wide range of subjects and explains a viewpoint on a topical issue giving the advantages and disadvantages of various options.

(Continued)

48   English language proficiency

English levels		Description of the language proficiency levels
	B1	• Understands the main ideas on a familiar context related to work, school, pastime, and so on. • Deals with a variety of situations that may arise when travelling. • Develops short and simple texts related to familiar or personal affection. • Describes his or her experiences and wishes. • Gives reasons and explains his or her opinions and plans.

	A2	• Understands sentences and uses expressions on his or her context.
		• Is able to:
		   ○ communicate in a simple context that requires a straightforward exchange of information on a well-known topic.
		   ○ describe features of his or her environment and background.

Basic	A1	• Understands and uses familiar workaday expressions.
		• Uses simple phrases to satisfy a need.
		• Is able to:
		   ○ introduce himself or herself and a third person.
		   ○ ask and answer questions related to personal information.
		   ○ interact in simple situations.

This table was developed by the author for the purpose of this book, based on information from the Common European Framework of Reference for Languages (CEFR) in its volume 2001.

Appendix C
Guidelines for the Implementation of the BIS Model

LINEAMIENTOS PARA LA IMPLEMENTACIÓN DEL MODELO BIS EN LAS UNIVERSIDADES TECNOLÓGICAS Y POLITÉCNICAS

I. Los siguientes lineamientos para la implementación de la Modalidad BIS entran en vigor a partir del ciclo escolar que inicia en septiembre 2014.

II. En la difusión de las Universidades BIS, deberá hacerse énfasis en que el conocimiento o dominio del inglés no es requisito para el ingreso de los alumnos.

III. Todas las áreas de la universidad deberán conocer con precisión las características de la Modalidad BIS.

IV. Todos los alumnos de nuevo ingreso deberán tomar un examen diagnóstico a través del instrumento: For Real Test, por ser un instrumento confiable y gratuito. Este mismo instrumento se empleará para evaluar el logro del nivel A2 al finalizar el curso propedéutico "Introducción a la lengua inglesa".

V. Se empleará el examen International Test of English Proficiency (iTEP) para certificar el nivel de dominio del idioma de los alumnos, correspondiente a cada título profesional que obtengan (B2 para TSU y C1 para Ingeniería) y para los profesores que no cuenten con certificación del nivel de dominio del idioma, debido a que ofrece las siguientes ventajas:
   a   es un instrumento confiable
   b   con reconocimiento internacional
   c   evalúa las cuatro habilidades lingüísticas
   d   se aplica en línea
   e   es de costo accesible
   f   cuenta con niveles equivalentes al MCERL.

VI. Las universidades deberán implementar las estrategias necesarias para garantizar que los alumnos logren el nivel de inglés que se ha establecido para cada curso. Aquellos estudiantes que no logren el nivel de inglés establecido en cada cuatrimestre, aún con las acciones remediales que la institución establezca, no podrá avanzar al siguiente cuatrimestre.

VII. Entre las estrategias para garantizar el logro del idioma se deben incluir las siguientes:
    a   Programar actividades en casa y en aulas, similares a las que se incluyen en el iTEP, con límites de tiempo como los establecidos en el examen.
    b   Programar tareas en casa que fortalezcan el aprendizaje independiente, relacionadas con las habilidades a desarrollar de acuerdo al nivel, con enfoque académico. (Academic Writing, Academic Reading, realizar presentaciones de lo leído/elaborado).
    c   Realizar evaluaciones periódicas para garantizar el logro de las habilidades lingüísticas acordes al nivel y con enfoque académico.
    d   Reforzar el inglés en las asignaturas técnicas, aún aquellas que no se imparten en inglés.

VIII. Los profesores que impartirán las asignaturas de inglés en el modelo de la Universidad Tecnológica BIS, tanto para el primer cuatrimestre, como para los cursos de TSU e ingeniería deberán contar con las siguientes certificaciones:
    a   Certificación Pedagógica en Enseñanza de Idiomas.
    b   Para impartir clases en nivel Técnico Superior Universitario: Mínimo nivel B2 de dominio del idioma de acuerdo al MCERL (iTEP, IELTS o FCE).
    c   Para impartir clases en nivel Ingeniería: Nivel C1 de dominio del idioma de acuerdo aI MCERL (iTEP, IELTS o CAE).

IX. Será requisito para los profesores que impartan las asignaturas técnicas de los niveles de TSU y Licenciatura, que estén certificados al menos, en el nivel B2 del MCERL. Lo anterior, además de los requisitos académicos propios de la disciplina a impartir que la universidad establezca.

X. El tiempo del curso propedéutico Introducción a la Lengua Inglesa, estará dividida en dos bloques para cada grupo:
    a   El primero constará de 5 horas al día, que serán atendidas por un profesor titular del aula y será responsable de reportar la evaluación.

b El segundo constará de dos horas diarias, que serán atendidas por un profesor titular de cada taller en las cuales se impartirán los siguientes talleres: Writing, Speaking, Reading, Listening y Grammar/Vocabulary.

XI. Los talleres deberán ser acreditados por el alumno para aprobar la asignatura.

XII. Las universidades deberán generar un glosario de términos técnicos en inglés para cada una de las asignaturas que integran el programa educativo, a partir del curso propedéutico.

XIII. Todo el personal de la universidad, docentes y administrativos, deberán de dominar el inglés y harán uso de el en todo momento dentro de las instalaciones, especialmente al dirigirse a los alumnos.

XIV. De acuerdo con el modelo, se deben impartir dos asignaturas en inglés durante el primer cuatrimestre, cuatro en el segundo y a partir de tercer cuatrimestre todas las asignaturas se deben impartir en inglés.

a Si las carreras a impartir ya se encuentran en la oferta de otras universidades BIS, la universidad deberá impartir en inglés las asignaturas de primero y segundo cuatrimestre que ya se acordaron por el Comité de Coordinadores de la Modalidad BIS.

b Si alguna carrera no se encuentra entre las ofrecidas por las Universidades BIS, la Universidad deberá informar oficialmente a la CGUTyP las asignaturas que se impartirán en inglés al menos dos meses antes de la apertura del programa.

XV. Los alumnos de nuevo ingreso que ya cuenten con un nivel B2 de dominio de la lengua inglesa, pueden optar por complementar su formación lingüística con un idioma adicional durante el cuatrimestre propedéutico, mismo que, preferentemente, deberá corresponder al idioma de origen de las empresas extranjeras establecidas en la región.

XVI. La universidad deberá proponer a mediano plazo un plan de acción para incorporar la sustentabilidad como uno de sus ejes rectores.

XVII. En la planeación cuatrimestral, la integración de los grupos de inglés debe realizarse por nivel de dominio y no por carrera. Se deberán establecer horarios fijos para las clases de inglés y realizar el resto de la planeación cuatrimestral a partir de éstos.

Appendix D
The sheltered instruction observation protocol (SIOP) model

The sheltered instruction observation protocol (SIOP)				
Components		*Observed*	*Not observed*	*Comments*
1 Preparation	Pays appropriate attention to both content and language objectives of lesson preparation and their fit with the educational background and language proficiency of students.			
2 Building background	This component involves making explicit links between concepts and students' background experiences. Emphasizing key vocabulary can also be included in this component.			
3 Comprehensible input	Refers to the various instructional strategies to make content accessible to students with limited language proficiency.			

The sheltered instruction observation protocol (SIOP)

Components		Observed	Not observed	Comments
4	Strategies	This component focuses on providing learners with information about learning strategies.		
5	Interaction	Focuses on opportunities for interaction and discussion and provision of sufficient wait time.		
6	Practice/ application	This component concerns the adequacy of hands-on materials so that student may apply content and language knowledge.		
7	Lesson delivery	Refers to whether content and language objectives are clearly supported.		
8	Review/ assessment	This component concerns how instructors provide comprehensive review of vocabulary and content concepts, assess students' learning, and provide feedback.		

The SIOP components. Sources: The Centre for Applied Linguistics (CAL), 2017; Park, 2015. Adapted for the purpose of data collection in this research.

Appendix E
Training opportunities offered by the UTR since 2013

PROGRAMME	2013	2014	2015	2016	2017	PARTICIPANTS
ALAMO COLLEGES VISIT	5					Students and professors
SEP—BÉCALOS—SANTANDER UNIVERSIDADES		165	39	61		Students in the Community Colleges of Nassau, PIMA, Fox Valley, Skyline, Alamo, Indian Hills, Broome, Fulton-Montgomery, and Central Seattle in the USA. This year we are participating with Canadian institutions like the Colleges of Centennial, Lambton, St. Lawrence, Georgian and New Caledonia colleges in Canada, and the Universities of Regina and Lakehead
CATT/TEFL (Content Area Teacher Training/ Teaching English as a Foreign Language)		12	7			Teachers in University of Arizona
Teacher Training in Canada				12		English Teachers and Associate Professors
PROYECTA 100,000		7	3	5		Students and teachers in the USA
PROYECTA 10,000			1			A teacher in Canada
SUMMER IN JAPAN		1	1			Students in Alamo College and Japan
SILICON VALLEY			5			Students in Silicon Valley
UCLA			1			Director of Academic Affairs, in developing women leaders in university faculty and administration

AIESEC		3	5	4	Foreign trainees in social and professional programmes
U.S. EMBASSY		1	1	1	Languages specialists through English language fellow programme
SEP		1	2	1	Teacher assistant in English and French languages
PROGRAMA DE INICIATIVA EMPRESARIAL, INNOVACIÓN Y LIDERAZGO, POR ALAMO COLLEGES			13		Students in a leadership programme in Alamo College
PEACE CORPS MEXICO			1	1	A volunteer from the USA
TESOL				1	Teacher in Baltimore/Seattle
UNILEAD GERMANY				1	Chief of the International Affairs Department/Director of Academic Affairs
MEXPROTEC				1	A student having a professional license
UNIVERSITY OF REGINA				4	Students and the President of UTR in a language programme
SUMMER SPANISH IMMERSION COURSE				3	Students from the University of Regina in a summer programme at UTR
INTERNSHIP PROGRAMME WITH AIESEC IN EGYPT				1	A mechatronics student in an internship programme working in BETCOM COMPANY
DEBRECEN UNIVERSITY IN HUNGARY				1	A student continuing his studies pursuing bachelor's degree
FOREIGN TEACHERS		1	1	2	Teachers from Puerto Rico, USA, and Haiti working in the languages department
TOTAL		6	191	79	99	2	377 INTERNATIONAL EXPERIENCES

Glossary

Agent of change A person who encourages and facilitates change or innovation in his or her profession (Havelock, 1973; O'connell Rust & Freidus, 2001; Varghese, 2004).

Autonomous A person or organization that is independent to make decisions.

Bilingual institution In Mexican higher education, the term *bilingual* is used to refer to those institutions that teach subjects in English.

Continuing Professional Development It is the development of a person in his or her professional role. CPD refers to in-service and long-term development of teachers, through programmes designed to facilitate teachers' self-understanding and reflection of teaching (Richards & Farrell, 2005; Villegas-Reimers, 2003).

Decentralized Units In Mexico, this refers to those institutions that belong to the Ministry of Higher Education, which are not controlled by the Administrative Units.

Descriptive statistics These are tools that help to organize and summarize data that come from studies of populations or samples (Holcomb, 1998).

Documentary source Newspapers, photographs, and documents that can be valuable resources (Gibson & Brown, 2009).

Extrinsic motivation External factors that inspire an individual towards doing or developing.

Focus group Is a technique used in social science studies. Focus groups may vary, but they usually include a semi-structured session (Carey & Asbury, 2012).

Future learn It is an online platform that offers a great number of Massive Open Online Courses (MOOCs).

Google Forms Along with Docs, Sheets, and Slides, it is part of Google's online free apps (Google forms, 2017).

Insider A person who positions himself or herself as an insider who can enable someone "to be closer to the 'backstage' behaviour, where people become more likely to do and say what they truly think and feel" (Goffman, 1959, cited by Leavy, 2015, p. 544).

Intrinsic motivation An internal desire that motivates an individual towards doing or developing something.

Monolingual Refers to an institution that offers education in a single language; in the case of Mexico, it is Spanish.

Problematizing Make into or regard as a problem requiring a solution (*Oxford Dictionary*, 2017).

Purposive sampling It is a research technique to select a sample using "…the expert judgement of the researchers…." The purposive sampling techniques are based on a "specific purpose" (Tashakkori & Teddlie, 2009, pp. 173–174). Some characteristics of the purposive sampling are as follows:

- Purposes are related to research questions.
- Informants are relevant for the selection.
- This sampling produces focus on the depth.
- Purposive samples are typically small (thirty or fewer; Tashakkori & Teddlie, 2014).

Semi-structured interview/observation Includes open-ended and theory-based questions that should be connected to the purpose of the research (Galletta, 2013).

Stimulated recall It is a call for reflection of practices by way of some kind of stimuli (Klaassen & Graaff, 2001).

Structured interview/observation It is a formal way of interviewing or observing. The structured interview or structured observation are followed by a well-structured set of questions that are developed in order to allow the researcher to lead the session. There may be certain instruments that are adapted from previous research to conduct a structured interview, or instruments may be developed by the researcher to fulfil the research needs.

Sustainability It is related to the use of resources that do not harm the environment.

Teacher training Encompasses the pre-teaching teacher education, usually established for short-term goals linked to present or immediate needs of teachers. Furthermore, teacher training generally involves theory and its application to teaching (Richards & Farrell, 2005).

Teaching school   In Mexico, this refers to universities that offer a bachelor's degree and postgraduate studies focused on the pedagogy of education to teach in kindergarten and primary schools.

The Blue Book (or el Libro Azúl for its title in Spanish)   It is in the argot of technological universities and a well-known document that presents the background to the implementation of technological universities in Mexico. It is an official document developed and distributed in the technological universities by the SEP in 1991. The Blue Book also discusses the mission, objectives, the pedagogical model, and the methodology for the implementation of technological universities in Mexico, as well as the ideal structure of the institution in administrative and financial terms. The 1991 Blue Book version can be accessed at: http://transparencia2.zacatecas.gob.mx/files/LIBRO%20AZUL2010.pdf.

Thematic analysis   It is a data analysis method that involves coding—breaking down data (looking for patterns), conceptualizing (labelling and grouping), and placing back together (Bogdan & Biklen, 1992; Mendenhall & Beaver, 2013; Tashakkori & Teddlie, 2009).

Triangulation of data   It refers to combining different sorts of data on the background of the theoretical perspectives which are applied to the data. Triangulation should produce knowledge on different levels, which means insights that go beyond the knowledge made possible by one approach and, thus, contribute to promoting quality in research (Flick, 2014, p. 184).

References

Bogdan, R. C., & Biklen, S. K. (1992). *Qualitative research for education. An introduction to theory and methods*. Boston, MA: Allyn & Bacon.

Carey, M. A., & Asbury, J.-E. (2012) *Focus group research*. London: Routledge.

Flick, U. (2014). *An introduction to qualitative research*. London: Sage.

Galletta, A. (2013) *Mastering the semi-structured interview and beyond*. New York: New York University Press.

Gibson, W., & Brown, A. (2009) *Working with qualitative data*. London: Sage.

Goffman, E. (1959). *The presentation of self in everyday life*. Garden City, NY: Doubleday.

Google Forms. (2017). Get started with Hangouts. Retrieved April 20, 2017, from https://support.google.com/hangouts/answer/2944865?co=GENIE.Platform=Desktop&hl=en).

Havelock, R. (1973) *The change agents guide to innovation in education*. Englewood Cliffs, NJ: Educational Technology Publications.

Holcomb, Z. C. (1998) *Fundamentals of descriptive statistics*. Los Angeles, CA: Pyrczak Publishing.

Klaassen, R., & De Graaff, E. (2001) Facing innovation: Preparing lecturers for English-medium instruction in a non-native context. *European Journal of Engineering Education, 26*(3), 281–289.

Kyriacou, C. (2001) *Effective teaching in schools: Theory and practice*. Cheltenham: Stanley Thornes.

Leavy, P. L. (2015). *The Oxford handbook of qualitative research*. Oxford: Oxford University Press.

Mendenhall, W., & Beaver, R. (2013). *Introduction to probability and statistics*. Boston, MA: Books Cole, Cengage Learning.

O'connell Rust, F., & Freidus, H. (2001) *Guiding school change. The role and work of change agents*. New York and London: Teachers College Press.

Richards, J., & Farrell, T. (2005) *Professional development for language teachers: Strategies for teacher learning*. Cambridge Language Education. New York: Cambridge University Press.

Tashakkori, A., & Teddlie, C. (2009) *Foundations of mixed methods in social and behavioral sciences*. Thousand Oaks, CA: SAGE.

Tashakkori, A., & Teddlie, C. (2014) *Foundations of mixed methods research. Integrating qualitative and quantitative approaches in the social and behavioural sciences*. Thousand Oaks, CA: SAGE.

Varghese, M. (2004) Professional development for bilingual teachers in the United States: A site for articulating and contesting professional roles. *International Journal of Bilingual Education and Bilingualism, 7*(2–3), 222–237.

Villegas-Reimers E. (2003) *Teacher professional development: An international review of the literature*. Paris: UNESCO International institute for education planning.

Index

Note: **Bold** page numbers refer to tables; *italic* page numbers refer to figures and page numbers followed by "n" denote endnotes.

autonomous universities 9

bilingual, international, and sustainable (BIS) modality 10–13; bilingual 10; in Blue Book 29; curriculum 11–13; educative pillars 10–11; EFL hours and subjects **12**; implementation, guidelines 49–51; international programmes 11; schema *11*; sustainability 11; technological and polytechnic universities 1
bilingual settings, professional development programmes 21
British Psychological Society 26

case study, EMI 21–29; data analysis 27–29; data collection and research methods 27; ethical considerations 26; participants and selection 23–25; problem statement 22; sociocultural theory 25; validity and reliability 26
Center for English as a Second Language (CESL) 37
classroom observations 28
Common European Framework of Reference for Languages (CEFR) 3, 13, 13n3
Content Area Teacher Training (CATT) 37–38
Continuing Professional Development (CPD) programme 9, 21, 40, 41, 43

data collection 18
decision-makers 22
Department of Higher Education (DGESU) 5
Department of Higher Education Professionals (DGESPE) 5
Department of Professions (DGP) 5

educative models 6–7
EMI lecturers 33; during the class 38–39; post-class period 39–40; pre-class period 38; professional development opportunities 40–41; professional development opportunities, BIS university 35–38; thoughts, ideas, and beliefs 34; training courses 35–38; using EMI within class 38–40
Engineering 6–7
English as a foreign language (EFL) 13
English as a medium of instruction (EMI) 1; case study 21–29; findings 32–41; pilot study 18–20; recommendations 42–44; in tertiary education 34
English language: familiarization of 3; social learning environments 3
English language proficiency 3; by CEFR 47–48; level 23, 33, 40
English language programmes: in basic, secondary, and tertiary education 1–4
English language skills 22

Index

English language teaching 32; at public and private institutions 33
English Language Teaching Programme 13n2
English Skills Reinforcement (ERC) 35

findings, EMI 32–41; personal and professional characteristics, participant 32–34
first BIS universities 8–10
focus group 28
For-Real Test 11, 14n6

General Coordination of Technological and Polytechnic universities (CGUTyP) 1, 5, 6–8, 29n3
Google Forms 29n1
Graduate School of Education (GSoE) 26

higher education (HE) system 1, 4–13; see also Mexican higher education (HE) system

International Standard Classification of Education (ISCED) 7, 13n4

marginalized communities 8
Mexican higher education subsystem 6–8; educative models 6–7; International Standard Classification of Education (ISCED) 7; technician professional (TSU) and engineering 6–7; technological and polytechnic universities 6–7
Mexican higher education (HE) system 4–13; TSU level 4–5
Mexican Technological and Polytechnic Subsystem 24
Ministry of Education (SEP) 7, 8
Ministry of Higher Education (SES) 5; administrative units 5

National English Level Certification (CENNI) 3
National English Programme (PRONI) 3, 4
National English Programme for Basic Education (PNIEB) 3

online surveys, EMI lecturers 27–28
online surveys, students 28

pilot study, EMI 18–20; findings 19–20; pilot methods 18–19
polytechnic universities 6–8; bilingual, international, and sustainable modality 10–13; BIS, Mexico 45–46; international classification of 7
Polytechnic University of Santa Rosa Jauregui (UPSRJ) 8–10, 18
professional development opportunities 24
protocols, interviews 18–19

questionnaires: interviews 18–19; lecturers 19, 23

semi-structured interview, administrative staff 28
sheltered instruction observation protocol (SIOP) model 52–53
short-cycle tertiary education 7
sociocultural theory 24
Spanish 38, 39
stimulated recall sessions 28

technician professional (TSU) 10
technological universities 6–8; bilingual, international, and sustainable (BIS) modality 10–13, 45–46; international classification of 7
Technological University of El Retoño (UTR) 8–10, 18, 29, 32, 35, 42, 44; EMI lecturers' position 32; training opportunities 54–55
training courses, lecturers 19–20, 35–38; class and laboratory observation forms 36; Content Area Teacher Training 37–38; CPD programme 43; English Language Fellow 35; English Skills Reinforcement (ERC) 35; induction course 35; international training 36–37; micro teaching 36; Peace Corps Mexico 36; pedagogy 36; replication course 36; teacher mobility programme 36; Technical English 35; technical terms, glossary 36
twenty-one BIS universities, map 2

University of Aguascalientes (UTA) 9

For Product Safety Concerns and Information please contact our EU representative GPSR@taylorandfrancis.com
Taylor & Francis Verlag GmbH, Kaufingerstraße 24, 80331 München, Germany

www.ingramcontent.com/pod-product-compliance
Lightning Source LLC
Chambersburg PA
CBHW051800230426
43670CB00012B/2371